Utter Nutter

UTTER NUTTER

Andrew Nutter

BANTAM PRESS

LONDON • NEW YORK • TORONTO • SYDNEY • AUCKLAND

TRANSWORLD PUBLISHERS LTD
61–63 Uxbridge Road, London W5 5SA

TRANSWORLD PUBLISHERS (AUSTRALIA) PTY LTD
15–25 Helles Avenue, Moorebank, NSW 2170

TRANSWORLD PUBLISHERS (NZ) LTD
3 William Pickering Drive, Albany, Auckland

Utter Nutter series produced for Channel 5 Broadcasting Limited
by Bazal Productions

Published 1997 by Bantam Press
a division of Transworld Publishers Ltd

Text copyright © Andrew Nutter 1997
Home economist: Caroline Liddell

Photographs copyright © Huw Williams 1997
Food stylist: Gillien Maclaurin

The right of Andrew Nutter to be identified
as author of this work has been asserted in accordance
with sections 77 and 78 of the Copyright Designs and
Patents Act 1988.

A catalogue record for this book is available from the British Library.
ISBN 0593 043073

Printed in Great Britain
by Butler and Tanner, Frome, Somerset.

To Mum and Dad
for all your help and encouragement

Acknowledgements

Especially big thanks are due to Frances Whitaker, Executive Producer at Bazal Productions, for giving me such a great opportunity with my TV series, *Utter Nutter*; Nick Stillwell, genius director of *Utter Nutter*, who is almost as crazy as I am; the back-up kitchen headed by my top recipe tester Caroline Liddell; and Paul Riley, Trevor Hambley, Lucy Eagle, Monica Murphy and all the production team who worked so hard to make the programmes a success.

And also to Broo Doherty at Bantam Press, who, with Frances Whitaker and Caroline Liddell, performed miracles in putting this book together.

Finally, thanks to all the staff at Nutter's for putting the restaurant on the map and making it one of the finest in north-west England.

You don't have to be a nutter to work with Nutter, but I dare say it helps!

Notes about the recipes in this book.

All measurements are based on the standard set of metric measuring spoons and the conversions are those approved by the Guild of Food Writers:

1 tablespoon = 15 ml
1 teaspoon = 5 ml

All eggs are medium unless otherwise stated.
Throughout the book all cream is whipping cream.

Contents

List of Illustrations

Introduction

On a balmy summer's evening on the Lancashire moors, fire-works soared into the night sky, lasers danced, and showers of sparks lit up the area for miles around. It was a celebration at Nutter's Restaurant, near Rochdale, an annual summer event to mark the birthday of the restaurant. The enthusiasm and excitement generated that night provided the inspiration for the *Utter Nutter* television series in which I would be able to combine my love of food with my passion for special effects. Several weeks later, after a few lengthy champagne meetings (my favourite tipple), the Utter Nutter concept was born, and, consequently, this book.

If you're fed up with cooking the same things every day of the week, I'll help you, using that extra Nutter twist, to trans-form those normal everyday recipes into ones that will become part of your repertoire for ever. Forget slaving away for hours at the stove. My recipes are generally quick, not too complicated, and easy to follow. If you've been put off in the past by lengthy lists of ingredients then you'll love these dishes. Forget spending lots of money and hours in the super-markets; a lot of my recipes involve raiding your larder and your fridge. And, with just that little spark of imagination, you've got a cracker of a dish.

The meals you'll find in this book are not only delicious, but bright, bold, colourful – and will really impress your family and friends. Throughout the book there are handy hints to make the dishes foolproof (well, almost!) and outrageous ideas for serving them up so they look fantastic.

Listed at the back of the book you'll find my utterly nutty menus, which you may like to try for a themed dinner party or on a special occasion. Whether it's the collection of dishes from the cool, jazz-inspired 'Black and White' programme, the fiery hot influences from the 'Flames' programme or that quick flourish where the 'Speed' menu will be right up your street, all the recipes are guaranteed to titillate your taste buds.

Whatever you choose I'm sure you'll enjoy making all of my recipes. After all, you don't have to be an utter nutter to want to cook from this book, but you'd be an utter nutter not to.

Utter Nutter

Appetizers

Nutter's Breakfast Treats

Crispy Bury Black Pudding Won-tons

Crostini with Three Toppings

Crispy Celeriac Crisps

Mini Vegetable Samosas

Prawn Toasts

Nutter's Breakfast Treats

SERVES 4

These open sweet black bacon and egg sandwiches are quick, delicious and so versatile. They can be served as a breakfast treat, a light lunch or as a pre-dinner nibble. You may not have come across sweet black bacon: it is back bacon that has been rolled in molasses and cured over oak chips. If you cannot get it, use smoked bacon instead.

1. Heat the olive oil in a small frying pan and cook the bacon until it is golden brown and crispy. Then add the sliced mushroom and fry it until it is soft. Add the garlic, season, and cook for a minute longer. Meanwhile, toast the rye bread. Then put the bacon mixture on top and keep it warm in the oven.
2. Halve the hard-boiled eggs and remove the yolks. In a small bowl, crush the cooked egg white with a fork and mix in the cream cheese, the mayonnaise, and a few drops of Tabasco. Check the seasoning. Toast the white bread, and spread the egg mixture over it. (Don't throw the egg yolks away – you can use them in my Garlic and Basil Paste on page 23.)
3. Take the bacon toasts out of the oven and remove the crusts from both lots of toast, then cut them into nice neat squares or triangles. Serve on hot plates.

1 tablespoon olive oil
8 rashers sweet black bacon, rinded
1 large field mushroom, sliced
½ clove garlic, peeled and finely chopped
salt and freshly ground black pepper
4 slices rye bread
2 hard-boiled eggs, peeled
100 g/4 oz cream cheese
1 tablespoon mayonnaise
Tabasco
4 slices white bread

Crispy Bury Black Pudding Won-tons

MAKES ABOUT 50 small triangular pastries

1 tablespoon olive oil

1 small onion, peeled and finely chopped

1 clove garlic, peeled and finely chopped

2.5 cm/1 in piece fresh ginger, peeled and finely chopped

450 g/1 lb black pudding, skinned and chopped

1 bunch spring onions, about 8, trimmed and finely chopped

140 g/5 oz chicken breast, boned and skinned

salt and freshly ground black pepper

25 g/1 oz butter, at room temperature

2 eggs

150 ml/¼ pt whipping cream

a little freshly grated nutmeg

a few leaves fresh basil, chopped

1 x 350 g/12 oz packet won-ton skins

vegetable oil for deep-frying

The ultimate dish from northern England with, of course, that Nutter twist. I use the famous Bury black puddings, although any black pudding will do, then combine it with lots of Chinese-style ingredients and a light chicken mousse. The mixture is wrapped in small squares of a thin Chinese pastry called won-ton skins. Most Chinese delis stock them frozen. The won-tons are great either as party food dipped in Chinese plum sauce, or as a starter with salad leaves and a tangy vinaigrette. Very unusual and extremely tasty.

1. Heat the olive oil in a non-stick frying pan and sauté the onion, garlic and ginger. When they have softened, add the black pudding and cook for about a minute. Add the spring onions and remove the pan from the heat so that they remain crunchy. Put it to one side to cool.

2. Take the chicken breast and blend it in a food processor with a teaspoon of salt. Add the butter and blend again. Now add an egg and continue to blend while you pour in the cream. Stop the motor from time to time and scrape the inside of the bowl with a rubber spatula so that everything is evenly combined.

3. Stir the chicken mousse into the black pudding mixture and season with salt, pepper and nutmeg. Finally, add the basil.

4. Lay out 6–9 won-ton skins on a clean work surface and place a spoonful of the black pudding mixture in the centre of each. Beat the remaining egg and use it to brush the edges of the won-ton skins. Fold each in half to form a triangle and press the edges firmly together. Repeat until all the mixture has been used.

5. Heat a deep pan of oil to 180°C/350°F. Fry about 6 won-tons at a time until they are golden brown, about 2–3 minutes. Drain and turn them out on to kitchen paper. Serve hot.

Crostini with Three Toppings

MAKES ABOUT 30–36 crostini

Much more to my taste than boring canapés. If you are going to pass them round at a party, have the toasts ready and the fillings made. When you want to serve them just shove on the toppings and send them out. Don't try to assemble them ahead of time or the toast will go soggy – and you don't want to be known for your soggy bottoms!

1. Cut the baguette at a slight angle in slices about 3–5 mm/⅛–¼ in thick – you will probably get about 36 slices. Put the garlic and olive oil in a food processor, blend briefly, then season with a little salt and black pepper. Brush the baguette slices on one side with the flavoured oil and arrange them on a foil-lined grill pan.

2. Place the pan under a hot grill until the crostini are golden brown, repeat on the other side, remove them from the grill and reserve until later.

3. For the first topping, mix together all the ingredients and season to taste. Do likewise with the second topping.

4. For the third topping, drain the goat's cheese and put it into a food processor, with the basil – reserve about ten of the best leaves to use as a garnish – the garlic and some seasoning. Blend until the mixture is a smooth pale green.

5. Decide whether you wish to serve the mozzarella cheese and chicken toppings hot or cold. If they are to be hot, pre-heat the grill. Pile each filling on to 10 crostini. Grill until the mozzarella has melted and the chicken has heated through. Spread 10 crostini with the goat's cheese mixture, and garnish with the reserved basil leaves. Use any leftover filling on the remaining toasts. Serve garnished with some mixed salad leaves.

For the crostini

1 slim granary baguette, about 30 cm/12 in long

1 clove garlic, peeled

100 ml/about 3½ fl oz olive oil

salt and freshly ground black pepper

mixed salad leaves to garnish

For topping 1

1 x 200 g/7oz pack mozzarella, diced

1 beef tomato, skinned, seeded and diced

a few basil leaves, shredded

For topping 2

50 g/2 oz smoked chicken, shredded

½ ripe avocado, skinned and diced

½ small cucumber, peeled, seeded and diced

1 tablespoon tarragon vinegar

For topping 3

2 x 120 g tubs fresh goat's cheese

about 20 g/¾ oz fresh basil leaves

1 clove garlic, peeled

Crispy Celeriac Crisps

SERVES 6

1 celeriac, peeled

2 egg whites

2 tablespoons cornflour

175 g/6 oz fine dry white
  breadcrumbs

vegetable oil for deep-frying

*These are great as a standby snack and make an unusual alterna-
tive to the potato crisp for serving with drinks.*

1. Cut the celeriac into quarters and slice it thinly, 3–5 mm/
   ⅛–¼ in thick.
2. Put the egg whites in a large bowl and use a fork to whisk
   them until they are slightly frothy.
3. Organize an assembly line of the cornflour, egg whites and
   breadcrumbs. Then dip the celeriac into each in that order.
   Lay the coated slices on a plate.
4. Heat a deep pan of oil to 180°C/350°F and fry the celeriac
   until it is golden brown. Drain on kitchen paper and serve.

Mini Vegetable Samosas

MAKES ABOUT 30 samosas

1 tablespoon olive oil

1 small onion, peeled and finely
  chopped

1 clove garlic, peeled and
  chopped

2 teaspoons mild curry powder

1 teaspoon peeled and grated
  fresh root ginger

1 teaspoon chopped fresh
  coriander

115 g/4 oz cooked potatoes,
  crushed

115 g/4 oz cooked vegetables
  (a mixture of peas, carrots,
  courgettes), chopped

few drops Tabasco

1 packet filo pastry

*A great way of using up leftover vegetables. Once made, the
samosas can either be fried straight away or kept in the freezer and
immediately deep-fried on removal, as and when needed.*

1. Gently fry the onion and garlic in the olive oil until softened.
2. Add the curry powder and fresh ginger and cook for a
   further minute or two before removing from the heat.
3. Add the coriander, cooked potatoes, vegetables and
   Tabasco to the curried onion mixture and stir until evenly
   mixed. Season to taste.
4. Lay the filo pastry out one sheet at a time, keeping the rest
   covered with a damp cloth to prevent it drying out and
   becoming brittle. Cut the sheet into strips approximately
   20 x 4 cm/8 x 1½ in.
5. Put a small teaspoonful of the vegetable mixture on the
   bottom corner of each strip. Fold this over so it forms a
   triangle, then continue folding the triangle over itself until

you reach the end of the strip. Stick the last turn down with a little beaten egg. Keep the samosas separate as they can stick together when they are damp with egg.

6. Heat a deep pan of oil to 160°C/325°F. Deep-fry the samosas for about 3 minutes or until golden brown. Drain on kitchen paper.
7. Serve with a little natural yoghurt or mango chutney.

1 egg, beaten
vegetable oil for deep-frying
natural yoghurt or mango chutney, to serve

Prawn Toasts

MAKES 20 (or 40 small) triangular toasts

You'll have eaten these in Chinese restaurants and had probably thought that they'd be hard to make. In fact, they are incredibly easy. On top of that, they can be frozen and deep-fried straight from the freezer whenever you want them. And you will want them.

1. Put the prawns on several thicknesses of kitchen paper and press firmly with additional sheets to soak up their moisture. Repeat with fresh sheets of kitchen paper until most of the moisture has been removed from the prawns. They should now weigh 150 g/5 oz.
2. In a food processor, blend together the prawns, egg white, cornflour, lemon juice, soy sauce, garlic and Dijon mustard until the ingredients form a paste. Season to taste if necessary.
3. Spread the paste thickly on the bread, as if you were spreading butter. Put the sesame seeds on a sheet of greaseproof paper then press the pasted side of the bread firmly into them. Remove the crusts then cut each slice into 4 triangles and in half again if you are making party food.
4. Heat a deep pan of oil to 180°C/350°F, and fry about 6 triangles at a time, turning them regularly until the bread bases are pale golden, about 3 minutes. Drain on kitchen paper and serve hot.

250 g/ 9 oz frozen prawns, defrosted
1 egg white
1 pinch cornflour
1 teaspoon lemon juice
1 teaspoon soy sauce
½ clove garlic, peeled
1 teaspoon Dijon mustard
salt and freshly ground black pepper
5 slices white bread
80 g/3 oz sesame seeds
vegetable oil for deep-frying

Soups

Cauliflower and Roquefort Soup with Jet Black Crostini

Celeriac and Asparagus Soup

Seared Cherry Tomato and Roast Garlic Soup

Lobster Soup

Mushroom Soup

Pea and Fennel Soup

Shellfish Soup with Garlic and Basil Paste

Cauliflower and Roquefort Soup with Jet Black Crostini

SERVES 4

If you can't get hold of tapenade, a cheat's version is to blend some stoned black olives to a paste with some olive oil and a hint of garlic.

1. Pre-heat the oven to 180°C/350°F/Gas 4/fan oven 160°C.
2. In a large saucepan, melt the butter and sauté the onion, garlic and celery for about 5 minutes over a low heat until they have softened but not coloured. Add the curry powder and cook for another minute.
3. Put in the cauliflower florets, the vegetable stock and the milk. Bring it to a simmer, then cover the pan and cook until the cauliflower is tender, about 10 minutes. Remove it from the heat and leave it to cool before blending.
4. Slice the baguette thinly into small rounds and place them on a baking sheet. Mix together the olive oil and garlic and drizzle it over the bread. Spread the tapenade thinly over the top. Put the baking sheet in the oven for about 5 minutes until the crostini are crispy.
5. Pour the soup into a food processor or liquidizer and blend it until it is smooth. Rinse the pan and pour the soup back into it through a sieve, then return the pan to the heat.
6. Now add the Roquefort and continue to heat, stirring, until the cheese has melted. Try not to boil the soup or the cheese will go a bit stringy. Taste and season, then serve it piping hot with the tapenade crostini floating on the surface.

For the soup

25 g/1 oz butter

1 medium onion, peeled and coarsely chopped

1 clove garlic, peeled and chopped

1 stick celery, coarsely chopped

1 teaspoon medium curry powder

225 g/8 oz cauliflower florets

300 ml/½ pt vegetable stock

300 ml/½ pt milk

60 g/generous 2 oz Roquefort, crumbled

For the crostini

½ granary baguette

2 tablespoons olive oil

½ clove garlic, peeled and finely chopped

1 jar tapenade (see recipe introduction)

Celeriac and Asparagus Soup

SERVES 4 healthy portions

1 head celeriac, about 400 g/
14 oz: 280 g/10 oz when
thickly peeled
1.2 L/2 pt chicken stock (see
page 110)
1 sprig of fresh thyme
1 clove garlic, peeled
150 g/5½ oz (about 15 stalks)
asparagus
salt and freshly ground black
pepper
2 tablespoons crème fraîche
1 tablespoon chopped fresh
parsley

You may have seen celeriac in your local supermarket and walked past it, not knowing what to do with it. Well, here's the answer, a soup with surprisingly few ingredients, but the flavour is awesome.

1. Take the celeriac and cut the root base away down to the white skin, then peel thickly. Cut into cubes. Bring the chicken stock to a simmer and add the celeriac with the thyme and garlic.
2. Remove about 5 cm/2 in from the tips of the asparagus and reserve. Cut away the woody part of the stalks, coarsely chop the remaining lengths and add to the stock. Cover the pan and cook gently for about 10 minutes, or until the vegetables are soft. Remove the pan from the heat and leave it to cool a little.
3. Pour the soup into a food processor or liquidizer and blend. Rinse out the pan and return the soup to it through a sieve. Return the pan to the heat.
4. While the soup is reheating, briefly cook the asparagus tips in salted water until they are only just tender, about 3 minutes.
5. Whisk the crème fraîche into the hot soup and check the seasoning. Serve the soup garnished with the asparagus tips and chopped parsley.

Crispy Bury Black Pudding Won-tons

Nutter's Soups: Seared Cherry Tomato and Roast Garlic;
Celeriac and Asparagus; Pea and Fennel

Seared Cherry Tomato and Roast Garlic Soup

SERVES 4

This recipe is great at any time of year, but in summer when the cherry tomatoes are so sweet and simply falling off the vine, it's sensational. Eat your heart out, Mr Heinz! If you haven't got one of those flat, ridged char-grills that go on top of the stove, use an ordinary frying pan.

1. Put an ungreased empty char-grill or frying pan over direct heat for about 5 minutes.
2. Meanwhile, heat the oil in a medium-size pan, add the onion, celery and leek, and cook over a moderate heat for 5–8 minutes or until they have softened and lightly coloured. Stir in the tomato purée.
3. Keeping your eye on the pan with the vegetables, put half of the tomatoes on to the char-grill and cook them until they are blackened and just starting to look squashy. Tip them straight into the pan with the vegetables. Repeat with the remaining tomatoes.
4. Finally, moisten your hands with a little olive oil and rub the garlic through your hands on to the char-grill. Cook it until it is lightly blackened. Add it to the vegetables.
5. Pour the stock into the pan. Strip the leaves from the basil, reserve them for the garnish and throw the stalks into the soup. Bring it to a simmer, cover and cook gently for about 10 minutes, or until the vegetables are tender. Leave it to cool a little.
6. Pour the soup into a food processor or liquidizer and blend until it is smooth. Rinse out the pan and return the soup to it, rubbing it through a sieve to remove the small seeds. Reheat it and taste: it may need just a little sugar adding to it as well as the usual seasoning.
7. While the soup reheats, shred the reserved basil leaves and serve each bowl garnished with some basil and a generous dollop of crème fraîche.

2 tablespoons olive oil

1 onion, peeled and coarsely chopped

1 stick celery, coarsely chopped

1 leek, coarsely chopped

2 tablespoons tomato purée

600 g/1 lb 5 oz cherry tomatoes

8 fat cloves garlic, peeled

600 ml/1 pt vegetable stock (see page 112)

sugar to taste

salt and freshly ground black pepper

2 large sprigs fresh basil

4 tablespoons crème fraîche

Lobster Soup

SERVES 4

2 tablespoons olive oil

the shell from 1 lobster, crushed – the finer you crush it the better

3 cloves garlic, peeled and coarsely chopped

1 onion, peeled and coarsely chopped

1 carrot, peeled and coarsely chopped

1 leek, trimmed, roughly chopped then rinsed

2 tablespoons brandy

375 ml/13 fl oz dry white wine

600 ml/1 pt fish stock (see page 111)

2 tablespoons tomato purée

4 beef tomatoes, chopped

15 g/½ oz mixed fresh herbs, thyme, basil, parsley, dill – any combination of these will do

2 egg yolks

150 ml/¼ pt whipping cream

salt and freshly ground black pepper

Use the lobster meat for my Lobster Thermidor Salad on page 34, then use the shell for this recipe – two meals for the price of one! Make this soup in the spring when English lobsters are at their best and a bit cheaper than usual. In case you're wondering how to crush the shell, I put it in a bucket and pound it with the end of a rolling pin. No bucket? Put the shell into a strong plastic bag and pound it with the length of a rolling pin.

1. In a large pan, heat the olive oil until it is very hot, add the crushed lobster shell and sauté it for 3–4 minutes or until it just starts to colour. Add the garlic, onion, carrot and leek, and fry gently until the vegetables have softened but not coloured.

2. Pour in the brandy, then the white wine, bring to the boil and cook for about 5 minutes to reduce a little.

3. Now add the fish stock, the tomato purée, the tomatoes and the herbs. Bring it to the boil again, then turn down the heat and leave it to simmer gently, uncovered, for 20 minutes. Taste the liquid: if the flavour is a bit thin, simmer the soup for a further 10 minutes. Remove the pan from the heat and leave it to cool a little.

4. Position a colander over a large bowl, then pour the contents of the pan into the colander and press down firmly on the shell and vegetables to extract the remaining liquid. Discard the debris. Rinse out the pan.

5. To ensure that no pieces of shell are left in the soup, pour it through a fine-mesh sieve into the clean pan.

6. Put the soup over a low heat and reheat it gently.

7. Meanwhile, whisk together the egg yolks and cream in a large bowl. Ladle about half the hot lobster soup on to the cream mixture and whisk briefly to combine, then pour it back into the pan and continue to heat, still whisking. Once the soup is just below simmering point and slightly thickened by the egg yolks, remove the pan from the heat. Don't let the mixture boil or it will curdle. Correct the seasoning, and serve with some crusty brown bread.

Mushroom Soup

SERVES 4, plus a refill

This recipe must be one of the simplest dishes ever and it's certainly one of the tastiest – that is, if you like mushrooms! It's even easier than opening a tin.

1. In a large pan heat the butter until it is foaming, then sauté the onion and garlic together until they are soft and tender but not coloured.
2. Add the mushrooms, stir to coat them with the butter, and cook for about 4 minutes. Now pour in the milk, add all the herbs and bring the mixture to the boil. Adjust the heat to a simmer and cook for 15 minutes. Leave it to cool a little.
3. Remove the rosemary, then put the contents of the pan into a food processor or liquidizer and blend until the soup is as smooth as it can get. Rinse the pan and pour the soup back into it through a sieve. Check the finished consistency. If you think the soup is too thick simply add a touch more milk.
4. Reheat the soup, and just before serving, whisk in the crème fraîche and season to taste.

50 g/2 oz butter
1 small onion, peeled and chopped
2 cloves garlic, peeled and chopped
900 g/2 lb button mushrooms, wiped clean then quartered
1.2 L/2 pt milk
a few stalks fresh parsley and basil
1 sprig fresh rosemary
2 tablespoons crème fraîche
salt and freshly ground black pepper

Pea and Fennel Soup

SERVES 4, plus a refill

1.2 L/2 pt chicken stock (see
   page 110)
1 potato, about 200 g/7 oz,
   peeled and cubed
25 g/1 oz butter
1 rasher smoked bacon, rinded
   and chopped
1 medium onion, peeled and
   chopped
1 bulb fennel, trimmed and
   chopped
2 sticks celery, chopped
2 cloves garlic, peeled
450 g/1 lb frozen peas,
   defrosted
about 4 sprigs fresh mint
1 tablespoon caster sugar
salt and freshly ground black
   pepper

To garnish
crisp bacon bits and crème fraîche

So that the soup remains bright green, blend it as soon as you have added the peas, or it will turn a murky brown – not exactly a gastronomic turn-on.

1. Pour the chicken stock into a medium-size pan, add the cubed potato and simmer until it is soft.
2. Meanwhile, in a large pan, heat the butter and gently fry the bacon for about 5 minutes.
3. Add the onion, fennel, celery and garlic to the bacon, cover with a lid and cook over a low heat for about 10 minutes, or until the vegetables are tender but not coloured.
4. Add the chicken stock and potato to the vegetable mixture, followed by the peas and the mint.
5. Pour the soup into a food processor or liquidizer and blend until it is smooth. Rinse the pan and return the soup to it through a sieve. Press the debris left in the sieve firmly to extract the remaining liquid.
6. Return the pan to the heat, stir in the sugar, then season to taste. Serve piping hot, garnished with a little finely chopped fried bacon and a drizzle of crème fraîche.

Shellfish Soup with Garlic and Basil Paste

SERVES 4

900 g/2 lb mussels, cleaned
25 g/1 oz butter
1 medium onion, peeled and
   finely chopped
1 clove garlic, peeled and finely
   chopped

If you're a shellfish fan then this soup is right up your street! The mussels will keep for up to 8 hours if stored in a cool place, wrapped in wet newspaper.

1. Scrub the mussels, removing the beards and any barnacles. If any mussels remain open after cleaning, throw them away, along with any that are cracked or splintered.

22

2. In a large pan melt the butter, then stir in the onion and garlic and cook over a low heat for about 8 minutes or until they have softened, but not coloured.

3. Pour in the wine and bring it to a fast boil before you tip in the mussels. Immediately clamp a lid on the pan and continue to cook over a high heat for 3–4 minutes, shaking the pan frequently.

4. Once the mussels have opened, remove the pan from the heat and strain the contents through a colander into a bowl. Discard any mussels which remain firmly closed.

5. As soon as the mussels are cool enough to handle, remove them from their shells and put on one side. Using a clean coffee filter or a sieve lined with kitchen paper, strain the mussel juice back into the cleaned pan to remove any tiny pieces of grit or shell.

6. Add the leek, potato, fish stock and saffron. Bring to the boil, then simmer gently, uncovered, for about 15 minutes or until the potato is cooked. Add the basil leaves and leave it to cool a little.

7. Put the contents of the pan into a food processor or liquidizer and blend until the mixture is smooth. Rinse the pan, pour the soup through a fine sieve back into the pan and reheat it, stirring in the reserved mussels, the cooked prawns and, finally, the cream. Avoid boiling the soup at this stage because overcooking toughens the seafood. Season to taste and serve with the Garlic and Basil Paste spread on crispy toast.

175 ml/6 fl. oz dry white wine

I small leek, trimmed, finely chopped and rinsed

I medium potato, peeled and finely chopped

600 ml/I pt fish stock (see page 111)

pinch saffron strands (optional)

a few leaves fresh basil

115 g/4 oz peeled prawns

4 tablespoons whipping cream

salt and freshly ground black pepper

Garlic and Basil Paste

A quick and easy sauce to serve with this shellfish soup, on crusty bread or crispy toast, or to accompany any fish recipes. In fact, it's brilliant for all sorts of things: dolloped on baked or new potatoes or practically any steamed veg, and great as a spread on crisp baguettes, crammed with salad, as a snack. Once made the sauce

2 hard-boiled eggs, yolks only

4 tablespoons good-quality mayonnaise

I tablespoon chopped fresh basil

good pinch turmeric

1 small clove garlic, peeled and
finely chopped

few drops Tabasco sauce

salt and freshly ground black
pepper

will keep in a covered bowl in the fridge for several days – and if you get hooked, the recipe is easy to double up. Use the leftover egg whites to make Nutter's Breakfast Treats (see page 9).

1. Crush the cooked yolks with a fork in a small bowl, then mix in the mayonnaise, basil, turmeric and garlic.
2. Add a few drops of Tabasco, mix and taste. If you prefer a hotter flavour just add a few drops more until it tastes right. Season with salt and pepper, if need be. It's as simple as that!

Starters and Light Lunches

Flash-seared Salmon with a Cucumber and Dill Dressing

Perfect Poached Eggs with Quick Hollandaise

Smoked Salmon, Crab and New Potato Timbales

Asparagus and Parma Ham Salad

Chicken Salad with Caesar-style Dressing

Goat's Cheese and Hot Potato Salad

Green Bean, Shallot and Basil Salad

Lobster Thermidor Salad

Pear, Avocado and Parmesan Salad

Leek, Cheddar and Tarragon Tart

Roquefort and Spinach Tart

Exploding Fritters of Oyster Mushrooms

Mille-feuille of Mushrooms and Broccoli

White Stilton Waffles with Tangy Rocket Leaves

Hot Skyscraper Sandwich

Goat's Cheese, Mango and Basil Fritters

Smoked Haddock and Spring Onion Risotto

Flash-seared Salmon with a Cucumber and Dill Dressing

SERVES 2

The dressing is flavoured with fresh dill, and in combination with the salmon and cucumber, this dish is hard to beat. What do I mean by flash-seared? Well, the salmon is coated lightly with flour then fried over a high heat so it gets a crisp brown coating while the inside stays moist and succulent. Serve it pronto with the cold, crisp dressing and maybe some pasta or new potatoes to make it a bit more substantial.

1. Make the dressing first by combining all the ingredients in a bowl. Taste and season carefully, then transfer it to the freezer to chill while you cook the salmon.
2. Have ready the seasoned flour on a piece of greaseproof paper. Heat an empty frying pan. Add the oil to the pan and wait until it just begins to smoke. Quickly coat the salmon with flour, shake off the excess and lay the fish in the pan.
3. Fry it until it is golden brown on the underside, then turn it and brown the other. This will probably take no more than 5 minutes in all. Don't overcook the salmon or it will become dry and tough.
4. Serve the fillets straight away with the cold dressing.

For the salmon
2 x 140 g/5 oz pieces salmon
   fillet, skinned and boned
a little seasoned flour
2 tablespoons olive oil

For the dressing
½ cucumber, peeled, seeded
   and finely chopped
1 large tomato, peeled, seeded
   and diced
1 red onion, peeled and finely
   chopped
2 tablespoons sherry vinegar
6 tablespoons olive oil
1 tablespoon chopped fresh dill
generous squeeze of lemon or
   lime juice
salt and freshly ground black
   pepper

Perfect Poached Eggs with Quick Hollandaise

SERVES 2 or 4

25 g/1 oz butter

115 g/4 oz spinach leaves, washed, dried, stalks removed

½ clove garlic, peeled and crushed

4 sun-dried tomato halves, drained of oil then shredded

freshly grated nutmeg

salt and freshly ground black pepper

4 slices white bread, cut into rounds with a pastry cutter

175 g/6 oz piece of black pudding, very thinly sliced

splash of white wine vinegar

4 very fresh eggs – they poach better

1 recipe Quick Hollandaise Sauce (see page 112)

Breakfast, brunch, lunch or supper – you choose. This recipe is a knockout: a toast base, covered with a layer of sliced black pudding, then a spinach and sun-dried tomato mixture, and finally, a perfectly poached egg, laced with Hollandaise sauce, balanced on top. Beautiful.

1. Put the oven on low: 100°C/200°F/Gas ¼/fan oven 100°C.
2. Heat the butter in a frying pan. Stir in the spinach leaves, garlic, sun-dried tomatoes, a little nutmeg and seasoning. Stir-fry for 2–3 minutes, then cover the pan, take it off the heat and keep it warm.
3. Toast the bread and lay on it the thin slices of black pudding. Put them on a baking tray and place it in the oven.
4. Pour about 5 cm/2 in water into a frying pan and add the vinegar. Bring it to the boil. Take a spoon and 'spin' the water clockwise for about 10 seconds. Immediately break an egg into the centre of the pan. The white will cover the yolk and set almost immediately. Leave it to cook for about 2 minutes, or longer if you like a set yolk, then lift it out with a large draining spoon and place on a warmed plate. Repeat with the other eggs.
5. Reheat the spinach, then tip it into a colander and drain off any excess liquid, pressing with a fish slice.
6. Arrange the black pudding toasts on hot plates. Top each with a flattened heap of spinach and arrange a poached egg on top. Spoon over the Hollandaise Sauce and serve.

Smoked Salmon, Crab and New Potato Timbales

SERVES 4

People will think you've slaved for hours in the kitchen to produce this dinner party starter.

1. You will need 4 x 150 ml/¼ pt ramekins lined with cling-film.
2. Line the base and sides of the dishes with strips of smoked salmon, leaving any excess hanging over the rims.
3. Put the crabmeat, potatoes, spring onions and chives in a bowl, gently fold in the mayonnaise and lemon juice and season to taste. Divide the mixture evenly between the ramekins, and press it down firmly. Fold over the excess salmon to cover the filling, then the cling-film, and refrigerate for about 3 hours or until thoroughly chilled.
4. To make the sauce, mix the yoghurt with sufficient lemon juice to give a sharp flavour, then add a generous grind of black pepper and salt to taste.
5. To serve, remove the smoked salmon timbales from the ramekins by gently tugging on the cling-film and inverting them on to individual serving plates. Drizzle with the yoghurt sauce and garnish with a few lengths of chives.

1 x 225 g/8 oz pack thinly
   sliced smoked salmon

For the filling
225 g/8 oz crabmeat, half
   brown/half white meat
175 g/6 oz new potatoes,
   cooked and diced
2 spring onions, finely chopped
1 tablespoon chopped fresh
   chives
3 tablespoons good-quality
   mayonnaise
1 teaspoon lemon juice
salt and freshly ground black
   pepper

For the sauce
6 tablespoons natural yoghurt
good squeeze lemon juice
salt and freshly ground black
   pepper

To garnish
whole chives

Asparagus and Parma Ham Salad

SERVES 4

20 asparagus spears, about
450 g/1 lb

1 perfectly ripe Galia melon –
it should *smell*

1 teaspoon Dijon mustard

1 teaspoon caster sugar

1 tablespoon white wine
vinegar

3 tablespoons olive oil

1 teaspoon chopped fresh
chervil

salt and freshly ground black
pepper

20 wafer-thin slices Parma
ham

mixed salad leaves

Make this dish when the new English asparagus is in season and you are definitely in for a treat.

1. Hold the bottom half of an asparagus stalk in both hands. Bend and snap off the end. It will break at the point where the tough, woody base becomes tender. Treat all the stalks in the same way, discarding the ends.

2. Cook the spears in boiling salted water for 3–4 minutes, depending on their thickness. Try not to overcook them – they should be slightly crunchy. Immediately they are ready, drain and plunge them into iced water. This stops the cooking and fixes the green colour. Drain and dry them on kitchen paper.

3. Cut the melon in half, discard the seeds, and use a melon baller to scoop out the flesh. Reserve in a bowl.

4. Use a spoon to scoop out the remaining melon flesh, and put it in a food processor with the mustard, sugar, vinegar, olive oil and chervil. Blend until smooth then season lightly – bear in mind that the ham is quite salty.

5. Roll each asparagus spear in a slice of Parma ham, leaving the tip showing because it looks better that way. Put some salad leaves on each plate, arrange the rolls on top, scatter them with the melon balls and drizzle over the dressing. Finally, grind black pepper generously over each portion and serve.

Chicken Salad with Caesar-style Dressing

SERVES 4

When you're the cook you can do anything, so the anchovies that normally go in a Caesar salad have been removed – because I hate them! In my recipe they have been replaced with warm, moist, tender chicken strips. It's a vast improvement and makes the perfect light lunch.

1. Slice the chicken into thin strips about 5 mm/¼ in wide and 2.5 cm/1 in long.
2. Heat the oil in a frying pan and stir-fry the chicken over a high heat until it is lightly browned but only just cooked. Transfer it to a plate and keep it warm. Clean the frying pan.
3. Cut the bread for the croûtons into 1 cm/½ in cubes. Here's a good tip: if you are using squashy fresh bread, put the slices in the freezer for about 20 minutes to chill and become firm. They will then cut far more neatly.
4. Heat the butter and oil together in the frying pan over a low to moderate heat, then add the bread cubes and toss. You will find that the bread quickly absorbs all the fat but keep the croûtons on the move, turning them over and over in the pan. Once the croûtons start to crisp, put in the garlic. After about 5 minutes of stir-frying, the cubes should be a good golden brown and very crisp. Turn them out on to kitchen paper and leave them to drain.
5. For the dressing, mix together the garlic, egg yolks and mustard. Now use a fork to whisk in the vinegar, followed by the olive oil. Season to taste.
6. To serve, pile the lettuce on to the serving plates and put the warm chicken on top. Drizzle over the dressing and scatter each portion generously with grated Parmesan and croûtons.

450 g/1 lb chicken breasts, boned and skinned
1 tablespoon olive oil
4 Little Gem lettuces, leaves separated and washed
about 75 g/3 oz freshly grated Parmesan

For the garlic croûtons
4 slices bread, taken from a large white loaf
25 g/1 oz butter
4 tablespoons olive oil
1 small clove garlic, peeled and crushed

For the dressing
1 clove garlic, peeled and crushed
2 egg yolks
2 teaspoons Dijon mustard
1 tablespoon white wine vinegar
3 tablespoons olive oil
salt and freshly ground black pepper

Goat's Cheese and Hot Potato Salad

SERVES 4

For the potato salad

4 tablespoons olive oil

225 g/8 oz cooked new
   potatoes, sliced

2 shallots, peeled and very
   finely chopped

1 tablespoon white wine
   vinegar

4 leaves basil, shredded

salt and freshly ground black
   pepper

For the goat's cheese croûtons

2 tablespoons olive oil

1 clove garlic, peeled and finely
   chopped

4 slices white bread

1 x 100 g/3½ oz round goat's
   cheese with rind

Moist, melting and moreish! What more could you want from this quick lunch dish?

1. First make the potato salad. Heat 2 tablespoons of the olive oil in a frying pan and turn the potatoes in it until they are lightly golden brown.

2. Add the chopped shallots, white wine vinegar, shredded basil leaves and remaining olive oil, then taste the mixture and season it. Cover it and keep it warm.

3. Now make the goat's cheese croûtons. Mix together the olive oil and garlic.

4. Use a plain pastry cutter to cut the bread into rounds slightly larger than the goat's cheese. Put the rounds on a foil-lined grill pan and drizzle them generously with the garlicky olive oil.

5. Trim the rind from the base and top of the goat's cheese, then slice the cheese into 4 rounds.

6. Toast the bread on one side. Turn it over, top each piece with a slice of goat's cheese and replace it under the grill. Toast it for a further 5 minutes or until the cheese is bubbling.

7. Serve on top of the potatoes, with maybe a simple mixed salad.

Green Bean, Shallot and Basil Salad

SERVES 4

An amazingly versatile dish that can be eaten cold or warm, as a salad, starter, or even a vegetable dish to accompany a main course.

1. Top and tail the fine green beans and cut into 5 cm/2 in pieces. Warm the olive oil in a frying pan, add the beans and fry them gently for about 3 minutes, until lightly cooked.
2. Turn up the heat and stir in the garlic and shallots. Fry for a minute or two, then remove the pan from the heat.
3. Add the tomatoes, lemon juice, basil and mozzarella to the pan. Stir, taste, season quite heavily, and serve.

115 g/4 oz fine green beans
2 tablespoons olive oil
1 small clove garlic, peeled and finely chopped
2 shallots, peeled and finely chopped
2 beef tomatoes, skinned, seeded and diced
1 tablespoon lemon juice
4 large basil leaves, shredded
50 g/2 oz mozzarella, diced
salt and freshly ground black pepper

Pear, Avocado and Parmesan Salad

SERVES 2

Combining pear with Parmesan may seem a bit bizarre, but it's rich, juicy and mellow – wicked!

1. Quarter and core the Conference pear but leave the skin on. Quarter the avocado pear, discarding the stone, and take the skin off. Thinly slice the pear and the avocado, and arrange attractively on two plates.
2. Scatter with the Parmesan cheese.
3. Mix the dressing ingredients together, drizzle over the salad, season with a little salt and freshly ground black pepper and serve – it's as easy as that!

For the salad
1 large ripe Conference pear
1 ripe avocado pear
30 g/generous 1 oz freshly grated Parmesan

For the dressing
1 tablespoon white wine vinegar
3 tablespoons olive oil
squeeze lemon juice
salt and freshly ground black pepper

Lobster Thermidor Salad

SERVES 2

650 g/1½ lb lobster

mixed salad leaves

For the hot brandy and mustard
   dressing

15 g/½ oz butter

1 shallot, peeled and finely
   chopped

½ clove garlic, peeled and
   chopped

1 splash brandy

1 tablespoon balsamic vinegar

3 tablespoons extra virgin olive
   oil

1 teaspoon hot French
   mustard

few leaves fresh basil, shredded

salt and freshly ground black
   pepper

To serve

mayonnaise (see page 113),
   made with lemon juice and
   lime zest, or 150 ml/¼ pt
   good quality bought
   mayonnaise with lemon juice
   and lime zest added to taste

Rather expensive but worth it as a treat for that special romantic meal. This dish takes all the ingredients of the classic Lobster Thermidor and transforms them into a simple yet really trendy summer salad.

Start by cooking a fresh lobster if you can bring yourself to do it, but if you can't, buy one ready cooked from your fishmonger and have him crack the claws and split the tail in half lengthways. Make sure that he gives you the entire lobster because, although only the meat is used in this recipe, the shell can be frozen then used to make my delicious Lobster Soup (see page 20).

1. Take the cooked lobster and remove the claws and knuckles. Crack the shells with a small hammer and remove the meat. Do the same with the tail but don't use a hammer; just press down on the shell and carefully remove the tail meat.

2. Slice the tail into thin medallions, place them on a plate with the meat from the claws and knuckles then refrigerate until you need them.

3. For the dressing, melt the butter in a pan and sauté the shallot and garlic for 2–3 minutes. When they have softened, add the brandy, vinegar, olive oil, mustard and basil, season and warm the mixture through.

4. If you want to serve home-made mayonnaise, make it now, or simply add the lemon juice to ready-made mayonnaise.

5. Lay the mixed salad leaves on a couple of plates, divide the cooked lobster between the two and drizzle over the warm dressing.

6. Serve straight away with the mayonnaise, some hot crusty bread and maybe your favourite hot potato salad. Eat – and you're in seventh heaven.

Smoked Salmon, Crab and New Potato Timbale

Mille-feuille of Mushrooms and Broccoli

Leek, Cheddar and Tarragon Tart

SERVES 4

Try to buy young leeks for this recipe and keep away from the tough, woody ones as they alter the taste of the tart.

1. Pre-heat the oven to 180°C/350°F/Gas 4/fan oven 160°C, and put in a baking tray to heat.
2. Roll out the pastry very thinly and use it to line a greased fluted metal flan tin, with a removable base, 20 x 4 cm/ 8 x 1½ in.
3. For the filling, heat half the butter in a frying pan and add the garlic, onion and leeks. Cook the vegetables over a moderate heat for about 5 minutes, stirring frequently until they have softened and any liquid in the pan has evaporated. Remove the pan from the heat, sprinkle in the tarragon, season and leave it to cool.
4. Spread the leek mixture in the base of the pastry case and scatter over the grated cheese.
5. Break the eggs into a bowl, pour in the cream and season with the salt, pepper and nutmeg. Beat everything together thoroughly, then pour it over the filling in the pastry case. Dot the top with flecks of the remaining butter, and bake on the hot baking tray for about 30 minutes or until the filling is puffed up and golden brown.
6. Serve the tart warm, rather than piping hot, with some mixed salad leaves tossed in a mustardy vinaigrette.

For the base
175 g/6 oz puff pastry
a little flour for rolling

For the filling
50 g/2 oz butter
1 clove garlic, peeled and finely chopped
1 small onion, peeled and finely chopped
2 leeks, trimmed top and base, halved and thinly sliced across
1 tablespoon chopped fresh tarragon
salt and freshly ground black pepper
75 g/3 oz mature Cheddar, grated
3 eggs
300 ml/½ pt whipping cream
a little freshly grated nutmeg

35

Roquefort and Spinach Tart

SERVES 4

For the base

175 g/6 oz puff pastry

a little flour for rolling

For the filling

25 g/1 oz butter

1 onion, peeled and chopped

1 clove garlic, peeled and finely
   chopped

175 g/6 oz leaf spinach,
   washed, dried and stalks
   removed

salt and freshly ground black
   pepper

freshly grated nutmeg

115 g/4 oz Roquefort

3 eggs

150 ml/¼ pt crème fraîche

juice of ½ lemon

50 g/2 oz Cheddar, grated

*What more could you want? Crisp pastry, a gooey cheesy centre
and enough nutritious spinach to keep Popeye happy for a week!
Any pastry trimmings left after you have lined the flan tin can be
used for the Mini Eccles Cakes on page 105.*

1. Pre-heat the oven to 180°C/350°F/Gas 4/fan oven 160°C,
   and put in a baking tray to heat.
2. Roll out the pastry nice and thin and use to line a 20 x 4 cm/
   8 x 1½ in greased fluted metal flan tin with a removable
   base.
3. For the filling, melt the butter in a large pan and sauté the
   onion and garlic until they are tender. Add the spinach and
   continue to cook until it has wilted. Transfer the mixture to
   a sieve and press it hard with a spoon to squeeze out most
   of the moisture.
4. Turn it out on to a board, season it with a little salt, pepper
   and nutmeg, then chop it coarsely. Spread the spinach
   mixture over the pastry base and crumble the Roquefort
   on top.
5. Mix the eggs and crème fraîche with the lemon juice and,
   maybe, some pepper. Don't add salt as the Roquefort is
   slightly salty.
6. Pour the cream mixture all over the spinach and Roquefort
   filling and scatter the Cheddar over the top.
7. Bake the tart on the hot baking tray for about 40 minutes,
   or until the filling and pastry are cooked through. If the tart
   starts to colour too much, simply cover with a sheet of tin
   foil.
8. Remove the tart from the oven and leave to cool slightly.
   Serve warm with some mixed salad leaves.

Exploding Fritters of Oyster Mushrooms

SERVES 4

An exciting combination of light, crisp mushroom fritters, drizzled with a tangy dressing. If you don't like mushrooms, replace them with courgettes, but dry them on kitchen paper before coating them with the choux pastry.

1. Beat the additional egg into the prepared choux pastry, and have ready a baking tray lined with kitchen paper, on which to drain the fritters as soon as they come out of the oil. Heat a deep pan of oil to 160°C/ about 325°F.

2. Make the dressing by whisking together all the dressing ingredients and lay the salad leaves on the serving plates.

3. Take each oyster mushroom – the large ones may need to be cut into smaller pieces – and coat all over with the choux pastry. Drop several at a time into the hot oil. Don't put them into a frying basket and lower them into the oil because the choux pastry will weld to the basket as it cooks. Left to their own devices the fritters will sink, then bob up to the surface. All you have to do is flip them over occasionally in the hot oil, so that they fry to an even golden brown, about 5–6 minutes.

4. Scoop the fritters from the oil with a slotted spoon and drain on the kitchen paper for a minute or so.

5. Serve the mushroom fritters on top of the salad leaves, drizzle with dressing and scatter with Parmesan. Serve straight away.

For the fritters

1 egg, beaten
1 quantity Choux Pastry (page 110)
vegetable oil for deep-frying
175 g/6 oz oyster mushrooms

For the dressing

1 tablespoon tomato ketchup
few drops of Tabasco to taste
1 tablespoon Worcestershire sauce
1 teaspoon Dijon mustard
1 tablespoon white wine vinegar
2 tablespoons olive oil

To serve

50 g/2 oz Parmesan, freshly grated
mixed salad leaves

Mille-feuille of Mushrooms and Broccoli

SERVES 4

For the pastry

250 g/ 9 oz puff pastry

a little flour for rolling

1 egg yolk

For the vegetable filling

25 g/1 oz butter

1 small onion, peeled and finely
chopped

1 clove garlic, peeled and finely
chopped

225 g/8 oz button mushrooms,
quartered

175 g/6 oz broccoli florets,
main stalk removed

For the sauce

50 ml/2 fl oz dry white wine

50 ml/2 fl oz white wine
vinegar

50 ml/2 fl oz whipping cream

115 g/4 oz chilled butter,
cubed

1 tablespoon chopped fresh
chives

1 tablespoon chopped fresh
parsley

salt and freshly ground black
pepper

What? Has Nutter suddenly gone posh using words like Mille-feuille? Who does he think he is? A nutter? But you've got to admit it sounds better than 'pastry sandwich filled with vegetables'. A dish that's great for vegetarians and looks really stunning. But it's very easy – trust me!

1. Pre-heat the oven to 190°C/375°F/Gas 5/fan oven 170°C.
2. Roll out the pastry to a square about 20 x 20 cm/8 x 8 in and 1 cm/½ in thick. Cut it into 4 equal triangular pieces. Put the pastry on a baking sheet, brush the top of each piece with the egg yolk and mark a criss-cross design on top with a small knife or cocktail stick. Bake for 10–15 minutes, or until it is well risen and golden brown. Remove from the oven and leave aside until you are ready to use it.
3. Now make the vegetable filling. In a small saucepan heat the butter, then put in the onion and garlic and cook until they have softened. Throw in the mushrooms and continue to fry until they have cooked through, which should take no more than 10 minutes. Remove the pan from the heat.
4. The broccoli should be broken into small florets, about the size of a thumbnail. Steam or boil until they are just tender but still with plenty of bite. Drain on kitchen paper, then add to the mushrooms in the pan.
5. Now for the sauce. Heat a small pan, pour in the white wine and wine vinegar and reduce by half. Pour in the cream and again reduce by half. You should have about 6 tablespoons of liquid left at this stage.
6. Now, over a low heat, whisk in the chilled butter, bit by bit, until it has melted and is thoroughly mixed. Do not allow this mixture to boil or the sauce will lose its creaminess and become thin and clear. Add the chives and parsley to the sauce, taste and season, then remove the pan from the heat.

7. Slice the cooked puff pastry in half horizontally. Briefly reheat the vegetables then divide them between each pastry base. Spoon the sauce over the vegetables then put on the pastry lids. Serve straight away.

White Stilton Waffles with Tangy Rocket Leaves

MAKES 4–8 waffles depending on the size of the machine

I have always thought waffles were complicated, but when I had to make this American favourite from start to finish in just 2 minutes on a recent cookery programme I soon mastered the art and discovered how simple they were. They can be savoury or sweet, but it is essential to have a waffle-maker, either electric or one that goes over direct heat.

If you can't get rocket, which is a tangy salad herb, a good continental salad mix will do just as well.

1. Sieve the dry waffle ingredients together into a bowl, then use a balloon whisk to gradually mix in the eggs and milk. Now whisk in the water, followed by the melted butter.
2. Heat the waffle machine and brush it with butter or vegetable oil. Spoon in three tablespoons of the mixture, close the lid and cook until it is golden brown on both sides. Use this first waffle to gauge the amount your particular machine needs. It could need more than three tablespoons to cover the cooking surface completely. So adapt the amount accordingly until all the mix has been used. Keep the cooked waffles warm in the oven.
3. Make the sauce: warm the cream gently and add the crumbled Stilton – don't boil it, or the cheese will go hard and stringy. When the Stilton has melted add the chives and check the seasoning.
4. For the salad, mix together the oils, vinegar and nuts and pour it over the rocket. Toss, and put a little salad on each plate with a waffle. Spoon the sauce over the waffles and serve.

For the waffle mix

350 g/12 oz plain flour

pinch of salt

1 teaspoon bicarbonate of soda

1 teaspoon baking powder

2 eggs

225 ml/8 fl oz milk

125 ml/4 fl oz cold water

120 g/generous 4 oz butter, melted

For the Stilton sauce

300 ml/½ pt whipping cream

120 g/generous 4 oz white Stilton, crumbled

1 tablespoon chopped fresh chives

salt and freshly ground black pepper

For the salad

2 tablespoons olive oil

1 tablespoon groundnut oil

1 tablespoon white wine vinegar

8 hazelnuts, finely chopped

about 60 g/2 oz fresh rocket (see recipe introduction)

Hot Skyscraper Sandwich

SERVES 2

For the potato layers
1 tablespoon olive oil

2 rashers smoked bacon, rinded and chopped

1 large baking potato, peeled

1 pinch cornflour

salt and freshly ground black pepper

15 g/½ oz butter

For the chilli tomato salsa
1 green chilli, seeded

1 tablespoon chopped chives

small handful coriander leaves

1 medium onion, peeled and roughly chopped

1 tablespoon white wine vinegar

juice of ½ lemon

1 beef tomato, skinned, seeded and diced

For the steak
4 x 100 g/3 oz fillet steaks

salt and freshly ground black pepper

15 g/½ oz butter

4 tablespoons mayonnaise

The ultimate sandwich – in fact it's actually thin, crisp layers of potato alternated with fillet steak, mayonnaise and chilli tomato salsa.

1. First make the potato layers. In a frying pan heat the olive oil and cook the bacon until it is golden brown. Drain, reserving the oil in the pan, and put in a large bowl.

2. Grate the potato on to a clean tea-towel, gather up the ends and squeeze out the excess liquid. Then put the potato and the cornflour in the bowl with the bacon. Season and toss everything together well to mix.

3. Divide the potato mixture approximately in half and each half into three thin, flat potato cakes. Heat the butter with the oil left in the frying pan and fry the potato cakes, in batches, pressing them out evenly as they cook. Use rings if you prefer. When they are golden brown, remove them from the pan, and drain them on kitchen paper.

4. To make the salsa, put the chilli, chives, coriander and onion together into a food processor and chop finely. Turn out into a small bowl and combine with the wine vinegar, lemon juice and tomato.

5. Season the steak. Heat the butter until golden brown and fry the steak on both sides until it is cooked – 2½–4 minutes on each side, depending on how you like your steak.

6. To assemble the Skyscraper, take a potato cake, cover it with a spoonful of salsa, top that with the steak and add a spoonful of mayonnaise. Repeat, finishing with potato on top. Then make the second skyscraper.

7. A taste explosion!

Goat's Cheese, Mango and Basil Fritters

SERVES 4 (makes 12 fritters)

For this recipe I use Chinese spring-roll pastry, which makes the fritters really crisp. Chinese supermarkets always stock freezer packs of this pastry, but if they are impossible to buy in your area, use filo pastry, which is available in most supermarkets, and serve the fritters as soon as they are cool enough to eat.

1. Lay the sheets of spring-roll pastry on the work surface and cut each one in half. Lay a basil leaf at the end of each strip.
2. The mango stone lies centrally and is long and fairly flat, so cut either side of the stone from one long end to the other. Take one side, peel and cut it into 12 slices. Reserve the remaining mango half. Lay a slice of mango on top of each basil leaf.
3. Season the goat's cheese and crumble it over the basil and mango. Brush the edges of each length of pastry with the beaten egg.
4. Fold over the ends to enclose the filling, then roll each pastry into a cylinder,
5. Heat a deep pan of oil to 160°C, about 325°F. Deep-fry the fritters for 3–4 minutes or until they are golden brown, then drain them on kitchen paper.
6. While the fritters drain and cool, make the mango dip. Take the remaining mango half and scrape off the flesh that surrounds the stone. Put the flesh into the food processor with the remaining dip ingredients and blend until smooth.
7. Serve the hot fritters with the cool mango dip.

For the fritters

6 sheets spring-roll pastry
12 large fresh basil leaves
1 large ripe mango, peeled
salt and freshly ground black pepper
280 g/10 oz fresh goat's cheese
1 egg, beaten
vegetable oil for deep-frying

For the mango dip

8 tablespoons orange juice
2 cloves garlic, peeled
2 tablespoons clear honey
2 teaspoons Worcestershire sauce

Smoked Haddock and Spring Onion Risotto

SERVES 4

25 g/1 oz butter

1 small onion, peeled and finely chopped

1 garlic clove, peeled and finely chopped

175 g/6 oz Arborio rice

50 ml/2 fl oz dry white wine

600 ml/1 pt hot vegetable stock (see page 112)

5 x 115 g/4 oz fillets smoked haddock, skinned and boned

300 ml/½ pt milk

4 spring onions, trimmed and finely chopped

a few fresh herbs, to garnish

I have never been a lover of kedgeree, but this I like . . .

1. Melt the butter in a medium-size, preferably non-stick, pan. Stir in the onion and garlic and cook gently until they have softened but not coloured.
2. Add the rice, turn up the heat a little and cook for a further minute, so that the rice has the chance to colour a little. Pour in the white wine and cook for a couple of minutes until the wine has all but evaporated.
3. Add just enough vegetable stock to cover the rice. Carry on cooking over a moderate heat, stirring frequently. As soon as the rice has absorbed the stock, stir in some more.
4. While the rice is cooking, take another pan, bring the milk to a simmer then poach four of the smoked haddock fillets for 5 minutes or until they are cooked through. Remove the fish and keep it warm, reserving the fish-flavoured milk.
5. After the rice has been cooking for about 15 minutes, chop the fifth, raw fillet and add it along with some more stock to the pan. Continue to simmer for a further 5 minutes, or until the rice has just cooked and the risotto is just moist enough to flow creamily. Add a little of the fish-flavoured milk for extra flavour, and the spring onions. Season to taste.
6. Serve the risotto in shallow bowls, topped with the cooked haddock fillets and some sprigs of fresh herbs.

Note: If you want to be flash, shape the risotto in a ring mould. In this case, adjust the amount of fish-flavoured milk added at the end.

Fish

Brill with Potato Scales and Tomato-scented Cous-cous

Poached Cod with Squid Ink Tagliatelle

Roast Cod with Oriental-style Vegetables

Haddock with a Red Pepper Crust

Triple Lemon Soles

Red Mullet with Fiery Hot Mango and Coriander Salsa

Herb-crusted Salmon with Champagne Sauce

Parmesan-crusted Salmon with a Mussel and Coriander Chowder

Roast Salmon with Griddled Courgettes and Sweet Tomato Dressing

Futuristic Fish and Chips

Brill with Potato Scales and Tomato-scented Cous-cous

SERVES 4

If you've never eaten brill, do try to find it. It's similar to turbot but cheaper, and I find it even tastier. Here I top it with a crisp potato layer, like fish scales, and serve it with tomatoey cous-cous, so there's no need for any starchy vegetables.

1. Pre-heat the oven to 160°C/325°F/Gas 3/fan oven 140°C.
2. Take the potato, cut it in half lengthways, then trim each piece into an oval using a potato peeler. Thinly slice the potato pieces across and dry them on kitchen paper.
3. Warm the vegetable oil in a large frying pan. Add the potato and fry to soften but not colour the slices. Drain the contents of the pan into a large sieve positioned over a heat-proof bowl. Scatter the potato with sifted cornflour.
4. Coat the brill fillets with seasoned flour, shake off the excess, and lay them on a sheet of greaseproof paper. Arrange overlapping potato slices to resemble fish scales covering the top of each fillet. Then use the flat of your hand to press the potato firmly on to the fish.
5. Heat the olive oil in a large frying pan. Use the greaseproof paper to flip over the fillets, one by one, on to a fish slice then gently ease them into the pan, potato side down. Fry two at a time to give yourself room to manoeuvre.
6. When the potato begins to tinge brown around the edges, carefully remove each fillet with a fish slice, turn them potato side up on to a foil-lined and oiled baking tray and put them into the oven for 10 minutes to finish cooking.
7. Meanwhile, prepare the cous-cous. Bring the vegetable stock to a simmer and add the onion, garlic, tomato purée, leek and carrot. Cover the pan and leave it to cook for about 5 minutes, or until the vegetables have softened.
8. Put the cous-cous into a heat-proof bowl. Pour the simmering stock on to the grains, mix, then cover with a plate and leave aside for about 5 minutes to allow the grains to absorb the liquid.

For the fish

1 large baking potato, peeled

150 ml/¼ pt vegetable oil

2 teaspoons cornflour

4 x 140 g/5 oz brill fillets, skinned

2–3 tablespoons plain flour, seasoned

1–2 tablespoons olive oil

For the tomato cous-cous

600 ml/1 pt strong vegetable stock (see page 112)

1 red onion, peeled and finely chopped

1 large clove garlic, peeled and finely chopped

2 tablespoons tomato purée

1 small leek, trimmed, finely chopped and washed

1 carrot, peeled and finely chopped

350 g/12 oz cous-cous

50 g/2 oz butter

1 tablespoon chopped basil leaves

1 beef tomato, skinned, seeded and diced

salt and freshly ground black pepper

9. Now drop small pieces of butter on to the hot cous-cous, cover it again and leave it to stand for a minute or two before forking the melted butter, the basil and the diced tomato into the mix. Season to taste.
10. Serve a mound of cous-cous on each warmed plate topped with a potato-scaled brill fillet.
11. It's brill-iant.

Poached Cod with Squid Ink Tagliatelle

SERVES 4

4 x 175 g/6 oz pieces of cod fillet, skinned
4 leaves fresh basil
1 clove garlic, peeled and thinly sliced
300 ml/½ pt vegetable stock
350 g/12 oz squid ink (black) tagliatelle
3 tablespoons olive oil, and a splash for cooking the pasta
1 clove garlic, peeled and chopped
1 small aubergine, skin left on and cut into diamonds
25 g/1 oz butter
50 g/2 oz Parmesan, grated

For the sauce
25 g/1 oz butter
1 small onion, finely chopped
180 ml/6 fl oz dry white wine
180 ml/6 fl oz vegetable stock
300 ml/½ pt whipping cream
salt and freshly ground pepper

Squid ink gives black pasta its colour. Supermarkets usually stock it, and certainly delicatessens, but if you can't get hold of it don't panic – any sort of tagliatelle will do.

1. Take each piece of cod and cut a horizontal slice through three-quarters of it. Tuck a leaf of fresh basil and a few slices of garlic inside, season and re-form the fish.
2. Warm the 300 ml/½ pt vegetable stock to just below boiling and poach the fish until it is cooked through, about 4 minutes. When it is ready, drain and put it on a plate. Cover and keep it warm.
3. Start making the sauce: in a small saucepan, heat the butter and cook the onion gently until it has softened. Add the white wine and boil to reduce by half. Pour in the vegetable stock and reduce by half again. Finally, add the cream and boil for about 3 minutes, or until the sauce has reduced to a good consistency. Season to taste and keep warm.
4. Have ready a pan of boiling salted water, add a splash of olive oil and the tagliatelle: cook until it is *al dente*.
5. While the pasta is cooking, heat 2 tablespoons of the olive oil in a frying pan then toss the garlic and the aubergine in it until they are cooked. Drain on kitchen paper.

6. Drain the cooked pasta, season it well and add the butter, the remaining tablespoon of olive oil and the Parmesan. Toss thoroughly to mix.
7. Place some pasta in the centre of each warmed plate, put the poached cod on top and pour around the sauce. Garnish with the aubergine and garlic.

Roast Cod with Oriental-style Vegetables

SERVES 4

Transform that humble piece of cod with this feast of flavours and colours.

1. Pre-heat the oven to 180°C/350°F/Gas 4/fan oven 160°C.
2. Make a few incisions in the skin of the cod and insert a sliver of garlic into each one.
3. Heat the olive oil in a frying pan, place the cod, skin side down, in the pan and fry it until the skin is browned and crisp.
4. Remove the fish to a baking tray and transfer to the oven to finish cooking, about 6–8 minutes.
5. In a large frying pan – or, if you feel the urge, use a wok – heat the sesame seed oil. Add the vegetables in the order in which they appear in the list of ingredients, stir-frying each vegetable for about half a minute before adding the next. The vegetables should be served crisp and crunchy. Remove them from the pan to a dish and keep them warm.
6. To the pan add the ginger, five-spice, sherry, soy sauce and sugar. Simmer gently while whisking in the butter, then season to taste.
7. Arrange the vegetables on warmed serving plates, top with a portion of fish and spoon the sauce around. Serve immediately.

4 x 175 g/6 oz cod fillets
I clove garlic, cut into slivers
I–2 tablespoons olive oil
I–2 tablespoons sesame seed oil
I red onion, peeled, quartered
   and separated into leaves
115 g/4 oz baby corn, cut on
   the slant
I bunch spring onions,
   trimmed and cut on the slant
115 g/4 oz shiitake
   mushrooms, sliced
115 g/4 oz mangetout, cut on
   the slant

For the sauce
I tablespoon peeled and
   coarsely grated fresh ginger
I teaspoon five-spice powder
I tablespoon sherry
dash of soy sauce
I tablespoon caster sugar
25g /I oz butter
salt and freshly ground pepper

For the fish

4 tablespoons balsamic
    vinegar
1 tablespoon peeled and
    finely chopped fresh ginger
4 x 175 g/6 oz fresh haddock
    fillets, skinned and boned

For the red pepper crust

1 red pepper, seeded
1 clove garlic, peeled
50 g/2 oz Parmesan
100 g/4 oz dry white
    breadcrumbs
about 1 tablespoon olive oil
15 g/½ oz butter

For the spinach sauce

25 g/1 oz butter
1 clove garlic and 1 shallot,
    peeled and chopped
125 ml/4 fl oz vegetable
    stock (see page 112)
125 ml/4 fl oz dry white wine
300 ml/½ pt whipping cream
100 g/3½ oz young spinach
    leaves, washed, dried,
    stalks removed
salt and freshly ground black
    pepper

For the fennel

1 tablespoon olive oil
25 g/1 oz butter
2 bulbs fennel, trimmed and
    sliced

Haddock with a Red Pepper Crust

SERVES 4

This is another really versatile recipe. You can serve the fish simply topped with the red pepper crust with a salad on the side, or, for a more substantial and colourful dish, work through the stages, serving with the spinach sauce and, if you like, the sautéed fennel. Either way it's a knockout!

1. Sprinkle the vinegar and ginger over each piece of fish. Leave for about 1 minute to let the vinegar soak in.
2. Prepare the red pepper crust by putting the pepper, garlic, Parmesan and breadcrumbs into a food processor and blending until a fine crumb is achieved. Drizzle in the olive oil and add the butter; they help to bind the mix.
3. Turn the grill on full and allow it to heat up. Line the grill-pan with foil and transfer the gingered fish fillets to it. Place it under the heat for about 2 minutes or until the fish is half cooked. Take it out, spread the fish with the red-pepper mix and put it back under the grill until the fish is cooked through and the topping has formed a browned crust.
4. If you wish to serve the spinach sauce, melt the butter in a pan and gently fry the garlic and shallot until they have softened. Pour in the vegetable stock and white wine and boil gently until the mixture has reduced by half.
5. Add the cream and return the mixture to the boil. Stir in the spinach and cook for 1–2 minutes until it has wilted.
6. Tip the contents of the pan into a food processor or liquidizer and blend until the mixture is smooth. Rinse the pan and return the sauce to it, season and reheat.
7. If you wish to serve the fennel, take a frying pan, heat the olive oil and butter in it, add the fennel and sauté for a few minutes until it has softened but is still slightly crunchy. Season with salt and pepper.
8. Place some fennel in the middle of each plate, top it with the fish and pour the sauce around it.

Triple Lemon Soles

SERVES 4

A lovely, light, healthy dish. You may not have come across this method of poaching fish, but don't let that put you off – it's dead simple and the fish comes out meltingly tender.

1. Since the fish takes so little time to cook, it is best to have the potato salad ready first and keep it warm, so start by melting the butter in a medium-size pan. If the new potatoes are big, cut them into chunks, then add them to the pan with the chopped lemon grass. Swirl them around to coat them in the butter.
2. Add the cucumber, tomatoes and basil. Season, then toss the mixture gently, and leave it over a low heat while you cook the fish.
3. Put 2 fillets on a large sheet of cling-film, season, sprinkle them with some dill, then with a little lemon juice and wine. Fold the long ends of the cling-film over the fish, then fold in the sides and press the packet flat to make sure it is sealed so that no water can get into, nor any juices escape from, the packet. Repeat the process with the remaining fillets so that you end up with 4 parcels of fish.
4. Half-fill a large frying pan with water and bring it to a simmer. Arrange the fish packets in the pan, and put a large plate or saucepan lid on top of the fish to keep the packets submerged in the water. Simmer gently for about 3 minutes.
5. Open the cling-film packages on to warmed serving plates so that the juice is released on to the plate. If, for any reason, the fish is still uncooked, pop it under the grill for a couple of minutes. Serve the fish straight away with the warm potato salad.

For the lemon potato salad
50 g/2 oz butter
225 g/8 oz new potatoes, cooked, skin on
1 stalk lemon grass, very finely chopped
1 cucumber, peeled, seeded and diced
2 beef tomatoes, skinned, seeded and diced
1 tablespoon shredded basil

For the fish
8 x 85 g/3 oz fillets of lemon sole, skinned
salt and freshly ground black pepper
some sprigs of dill
juice of ½ lemon
about 50 ml/2 fl oz dry white wine

Red Mullet with Fiery Hot Mango and Coriander Salsa

SERVES 4

4 x 140 g/5 oz red mullet
fillets, all bones and scales
removed, skin left on

2 tablespoons olive oil

1 fresh green chilli, seeded and
very finely chopped

For the salsa

1 cucumber, skinned, seeded
and finely chopped

1 fresh red chilli, seeded and
very finely chopped

1 ripe mango, peeled and
chopped

1 tablespoon chopped fresh
coriander leaves

1 small onion, peeled and finely
chopped

juice of 1 lime

1 tablespoon white wine
vinegar

salt

For the sauce

1 small ripe mango, flesh
removed

1 tablespoon clear honey

1 clove garlic, peeled and
chopped

4 tablespoons fresh orange juice

Fed up with cod, haddock and salmon? Why not try red mullet for a change? It is available from most good fishmongers. This recipe is Thai-influenced, and although the salsa is hot, it is moderated by the exotic fruitiness of the mango. The two enhance the flavour of the fish. The recipe is ideal for a barbecue – so when you see a break in the clouds, rush out and light the fire, then come in and marinate the fish. By the time the embers are at the right stage for cooking, the fish will be perfectly marinated.

1. Marinate the fish. Combine the oil and half the chopped green chilli in a dish. Turn the fish fillets in the oil and leave for about 1 hour.

2. Make the salsa: Mix all the ingredients except the salt together in a bowl, including the remaining half of the chopped green chilli. Taste, season with a little salt, and chill.

3. Make the sauce: Combine all the ingredients in a food processor and blend until smooth. Season to taste.

4. Barbecue, char-grill or pan-fry the fish fillets – whichever way you cook them you will not need any additional oil as the fillets are coated in sufficient to fry them. Cook for 2–3 minutes on each side, skin side first.

5. Serve straight away with the chilled salsa and the mango sauce.

Parmesan-crusted Salmon with a Mussel and Coriander Chowder

Futuristic Fish and Chips

Herb-crusted Salmon with Champagne Sauce

SERVES 4

Now, look, don't panic. If you can't afford champagne, use a dry white wine. This is the ultimate dish for salmon lovers or even just lovers!

1. Pre-heat the oven to 160°C/325°F/Gas 3/fan oven 140°C.
2. Get the splash of olive oil good and hot in a frying pan then briefly fry the salmon on both sides until golden brown.
3. While the fish is frying, you can blend the breadcrumbs, herbs, garlic and Parmesan in a food processor until you have something like a green powder. Then add the olive oil and butter, and blend again until it is well mixed.
4. Use a fish slice to transfer the fillets to a baking tray. Pat some of the herb crumb on top of each then bake for about 5 minutes to finish cooking.
5. While that's going on, you can make the sauce. Melt the butter in a pan and sauté the onion and garlic until they begin to soften. (It's really quick, this recipe!) Now pour in the champagne and let it bubble until the liquid has reduced by half. Add the fish stock and reduce it again by half.
6. Next add the cream and simmer for about 2 minutes until you have a nice sauce consistency. Stir in the tomato and chives and season to taste.
7. Serve the salmon with the sauce and maybe a selection of fresh market vegetables and new Jersey potatoes. A blinder, this recipe, and as I've said before, dead quick.

4 x 175 g/6 oz salmon fillets, skinned and boned
splash of olive oil

For the herb crust
85 g/3 oz dry white bread-crumbs
50 g/2 oz combined fresh parsley, basil and dill
1 clove garlic, peeled
50 g/2 oz Parmesan, freshly grated
1 tablespoon olive oil
25 g/1 oz butter

For the Champagne Sauce
25 g/1 oz butter
1 small onion, peeled and chopped
2 cloves garlic, peeled and chopped
125 ml/4 fl oz champagne (see recipe introduction)
125 ml/4 fl oz fish stock (see page 111)
300 ml/½ pt whipping cream
1 beef tomato, skinned, seeded and diced
1 tablespoon chopped fresh chives

Parmesan-crusted Salmon with a Mussel and Coriander Chowder

SERVES 4

4 x 175 g/6 oz salmon fillets,
  skinned and boned
salt and freshly ground black
  pepper
small bunch fresh coriander
1 tablespoon olive oil
25 g/1 oz freshly grated
  Parmesan

For the mussel chowder
1 kg/2 lb mussels, cleaned
1 tablespoon olive oil
1 rasher smoked bacon, rinded
  and chopped
1 onion, peeled and finely
  chopped
1 clove garlic, peeled and finely
  chopped
200 ml/7 fl oz dry white wine
1 carrot, peeled and finely
  diced
1 leek, trimmed, finely diced
  and washed
1 potato, peeled and finely
  diced
200 ml/7 fl oz whipping cream
1 tablespoon chopped fresh
  coriander

My dream fish dish: perfectly moist salmon topped with melting Parmesan, served on a pool of creamy bacon and mussel sauce. Follow this recipe and you won't just be dreaming – you'll be in heaven.

1. Pre-heat the oven to 150°C/300°F/Gas 2/fan oven 130°C.
2. Make a horizontal cut half-way into each salmon fillet. Lift the top flap, season under it with salt and pepper, lay on a few leaves of coriander and re-form the fillet.
3. Heat a frying pan and put in the olive oil. Seal the salmon on both sides until it is golden brown. Sprinkle the fish with Parmesan, put it on a baking sheet and bake in the oven for about 10 minutes, or until the fish is cooked through.
4. Now for the mussel chowder. Clean the mussels as explained on page 22. Heat the olive oil in a saucepan. Add the bacon and fry until it is golden brown. Then put in the onion and garlic and cook, until slightly softened, for 3–4 minutes. Add the mussels – discard any open ones – to the saucepan, pour in the white wine, cover, and leave to cook for 2–3 minutes, shaking the pan occasionally until the mussels have opened. Remove them with a slotted spoon, discarding any that are still closed. Keep them warm.
5. Add the carrot, leek and potato to the white wine and mussel juices in the saucepan and cook until the vegetables are tender, for 10–12 minutes.
6. Now pour in the cream and bring to the boil. Add the chopped coriander, then return the mussels to the pan and warm through until they are sufficiently hot to serve. Over-cooking the mussels at this stage, though, will toughen them.
7. Serve the chunky mussel chowder around the Parmesan-crusted salmon in large soup bowls. It's orgasmic!

Roast Salmon with Griddled Courgettes and Sweet Tomato Dressing

SERVES 4

For this recipe I like to use a ridged char-grill pan, which gives the food a char-grilled/barbecued look, but the dish can be made just as successfully using a standard frying pan.

1. Pre-heat the oven to 160°C/325°F/Gas 3/fan oven 140°C.
2. Combine the olive oil and garlic in a food processor and blend briefly to chop the garlic finely. Arrange the fish on a foil-lined baking tray and drizzle a little of the garlic-oil over each piece.
3. Put the char-grill or frying pan over a moderate to high heat and leave it for a minute or more depending on the thickness of the pan until it is thoroughly hot. Put the salmon on to the hot pan, skin side down, and leave to cook for 2 minutes without moving. Use a fish slice to turn the fillets, then cook them on the other side for another 2 minutes.
4. Put the fish back on the foil-lined baking tray then into the oven for 10 minutes.
5. Meanwhile clean the char-grill or frying pan and re-heat it. Toss the sliced courgettes in a little of the garlic-oil, season, and tip them on to the pan. Fry them until browned but still crunchy, then remove them from the pan.
6. Add the basil to the garlic-oil remaining in the food processor, season, then blend until you have a green sauce.
7. Mix together the sun-dried tomatoes, sugar and vinegar, season to taste and put on one side.
8. Now to assemble your masterpiece! Line up the warmed serving plates and arrange the 3 tomato quarters in an expanded trefoil pattern in the centre of each plate. Put courgette slices between the tomato sections then pile any leftover courgettes in the centre. Lay the salmon fillets on top and pile the sun-dried tomato dressing on the

150 ml/¼ pt olive oil

I clove garlic, peeled

4 x 175 g/6 oz salmon fillets, with the skin on

3 thumb-thick courgettes, trimmed then sliced 1 cm/½ in thick

small bunch fresh basil

salt and freshly ground black pepper

75 g/3 oz sun-dried tomatoes in olive oil, drained and finely chopped

I teaspoon sugar

I tablespoon balsamic vinegar

3 beef tomatoes, skinned, seeded and quartered

nasturtium or pansy petals (optional)

salmon. Finally, spoon the basil oil around the plates. For the truly Nutter flourish, scatter with the flower petals. These are not just for effect – they have a distinctive, peppery flavour, which is just right with this dish.

Futuristic Fish and Chips

SERVES 4

4 large baking potatoes, peeled

vegetable oil for deep-frying

4 x 140 g/5 oz pieces skate,
   skinned, boned and seasoned

50 g/2 oz plain flour

For the batter

225 g/8 oz self-raising flour

1 teaspoon bicarbonate of soda

300 ml/½ pt water

1 teaspoon white wine vinegar

4 tablespoons Guinness or
   stout

1 tablespoon peeled and finely
   chopped fresh ginger

For the salt and vinegar sauce

4 tablespoons white wine
   vinegar

4 tablespoons malt vinegar

4 tablespoons white wine

8 tablespoons whipping cream

175 g/6 oz salted butter, cubed

2 tablespoons chopped fresh
   chives

This version of fish and chips transforms a humble dish into one that is simply out of this world. The combination of gingery, beer-battered fish with the salt and vinegar sauce is a knockout.

1. Cut the potatoes into chips measuring about 1 x 5 cm/ ½ x 2 in and dry them thoroughly. Heat a deep pan of oil to 140°C/275°F and deep-fry the chips for about 4 minutes until they are soft but scarcely coloured. Drain and reserve them. Increase the oil temperature to 160°C/325°F.

2. Make the batter: Sift the self-raising flour and bicarbonate of soda into a bowl. Mix together the water, vinegar, Guinness and ginger, and pour it into the flour. Use a balloon whisk to combine the mixture to a smooth batter.

3. Dust the skate with the flour, coat it in the batter and lower the pieces into the oil. (Do not use a frying basket as the cooked batter will weld to it.) Fry the fish for 4–5 minutes until it is a deep golden brown. Drain and put it on a baking tray lined with kitchen paper and keep it warm in a low oven. Lower the oil temperature to 150°C/300°F.

4. Now make the sauce. Combine the vinegars and white wine in a saucepan and boil until the liquid has reduced by half. Add the cream and boil again, to reduce until you have about 180 ml/6 fl oz left. Now put in the butter, a cube at a time, whisking each piece until it melts before adding the next. Don't let the sauce boil or it will separate. Finally, stir in the chives, taste – the flavour should be quite sharp – and correct the seasoning. Take the sauce off the heat and keep it warm.

5. Re-fry the chips until they are golden brown and crisp. Drain them thoroughly, then stack them in futuristic towers on each plate.
6. Quickly put a piece of battered fish on top of each tower, pour the sauce around it and serve.

Note: I serve fish in this manner in the restaurant because my customers prefer their fish without bones. However, don't attempt to prepare skate in this way unless it is *very* fresh.

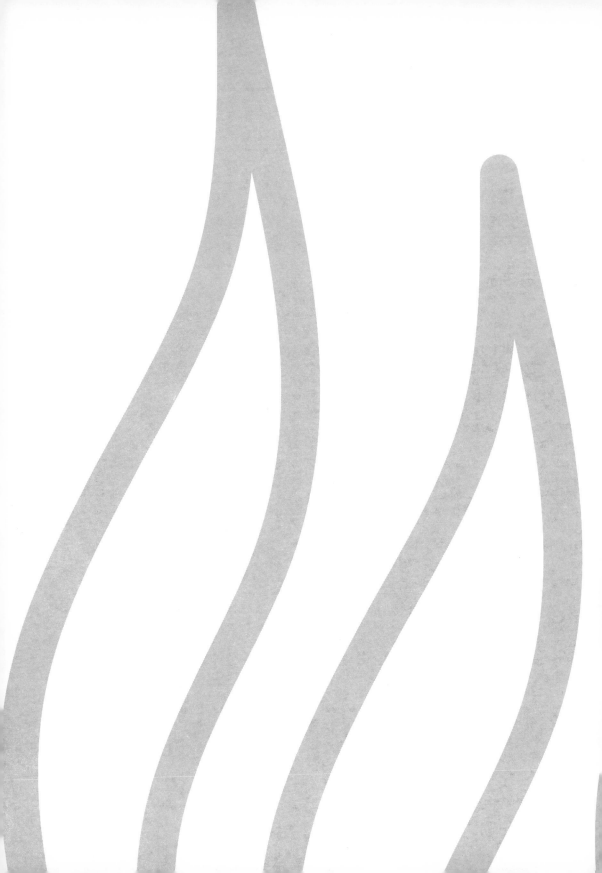

Meat

Chicken Breast with Creamy Lentils

Chicken with Fresh Ginger and Spring Onions

Poached Chicken Breast with Knockout Noodles

Poached Chicken with a Port Wine Sauce

Nutter's Oriental Bird

Chicken with Coconut Curried Cous-cous

Dazzling Duck Breast with a Honey and Mustard Glaze

Char-grilled Duck Legs with Barbecued Potatoes and Spicy Chorizo Sausage

Medallions of Pork with a Mushroom Risotto

Pork Pieces with Melting Stilton and Chive Fondue

Thai-style Pork Medallions

Lamb Cutlets with Caramelized Roast Vegetables

Medallions of Lamb with Creamy Cabbage

Peppered Steak with Mushroom Mash

Chicken Breast with Creamy Lentils

SERVES 4

The lentils I use in this recipe are unusual, but they have the best flavour of all. A lot of large supermarkets keep them, but if you can't get hold of them, use the slightly larger, khaki-coloured lentils – not the orange ones, which cook into a thick sludge as soon as your back is turned!

2 tablespoons olive oil

4 x 175 g/6 oz chicken breasts, with skin

1 large clove garlic, peeled and sliced

For the creamy lentils

50 g/2 oz butter

4 rashers smoked back bacon, rinded and cut into thin strips

1 medium onion, peeled and finely chopped

1 clove garlic, peeled and finely chopped

225 g/8 oz Puy lentils, rinsed in cold water and drained

1 carrot, peeled and finely chopped

1 bay leaf

600 ml/1 pt chicken stock (see page 110)

6 tablespoons cream

1. Heat the olive oil in a frying pan, lay the chicken breasts, skin side down, in it and leave them to cook over a moderate heat for about 5 minutes, or until they are golden brown and crisp underneath. Turn the chicken, then reduce the heat to low before you add the sliced garlic. Let the chicken cook very gently for about 20 minutes, basting frequently with the garlicky olive oil.

2. Now for the lentils. In a medium-size pan heat the butter and fry the bacon until it is lightly browned. Stir in the onion and garlic, and cook for about 5 minutes over a moderate heat until they are softened and lightly browned.

3. Stir in the lentils, carrot, bay leaf and stock, bring to the boil and adjust the heat to a simmer. Cook the mixture, uncovered, for about 20 minutes, or until the lentils are just tender. What you are aiming for is to have the lentils just cooked and most of the stock absorbed or evaporated.

4. Add the cream and bring the lentil mixture back to the boil. Season to taste and discard the bay leaf.

5. Serve the chicken breasts with the creamy lentils, and some steamed vegetables, dressed simply with melted butter.

Chicken with Fresh Ginger and Spring Onions

SERVES 4

3 tablespoons olive oil

4 x 175 g/6 oz chicken breasts,
with skin

1 bunch spring onions,
trimmed and finely chopped

2.5 cm/1 in cube fresh ginger,
peeled and finely chopped

salt and freshly ground black
pepper

For the stir-fried vegetables

2 large baking potatoes, peeled

2 tablespoons olive oil

1 clove garlic, peeled and finely
chopped

225 g/8 oz mangetout, topped,
tailed and shredded

For the sauce

125 ml/4 fl oz dry white wine

125 ml/4 fl oz chicken stock
(see page 110)

125 ml/4 fl oz whipping cream

2.5 cm/1 in cube fresh ginger,
peeled and finely chopped

1 bunch spring onions,
trimmed and finely chopped

One of my all-time favourite dishes. Not only is it really tasty, but it also won me the runner-up title in a national cookery competition – and that was when Nutter was thirteen! Nowadays I sometimes make this dish even quicker. If you cut the raw chicken in thin strips and sauté them with the ginger and spring onions it becomes a quick stir-fry that avoids having to heat the oven.

1. Pre-heat the oven to 160°C/325°F/Gas 3/fan oven 140°C.
2. Heat 2 tablespoons of the oil in a frying pan over a moderate to high heat and cook the chicken breasts just until they are golden brown outside but still raw in the centre. Remove them to a plate and leave them to cool a little.
3. Add another tablespoon of oil to the pan, then stir in the onions and ginger. Gently fry for 5 minutes, until they have softened but not coloured. Remove the pan from the heat and season lightly.
4. Using a sharp knife, make 4 oblique cuts, evenly spaced, to the centre of each chicken breast. Push a little of the onion and ginger mixture into each cut so that the flavours penetrate well into the meat.
5. Transfer the chicken to a foil-lined baking tray and bake for a further 10–12 minutes, or until it is cooked through.
6. Meanwhile, dice the potatoes in 1 cm/½ in pieces then dry on kitchen paper. Heat the olive oil in a frying pan and sauté the diced potato until it is golden brown and tender. Add the garlic and mangetout, and continue to sauté for a minute or two. Cover and keep warm.
7. For the sauce, pour the wine into a small pan and reduce it by half. Add the chicken stock and reduce by half again before stirring in the cream, the ginger and the spring onions. Bring the mixture to a simmer and season to taste.
8. Serve each chicken breast on a bed of the stir-fried vegetables with the sauce spooned over the chicken.

60

Poached Chicken Breast with Knockout Noodles

SERVES 4

Delicately poached chicken breasts become exciting with a hot, tangy dressing and my exotic knockout noodles.

1. Take a large saucepan, pour in the stock and bring it to the boil. Place the chicken breasts in the stock and simmer gently until they are tender and cooked through, about 10 minutes.
2. Meanwhile, make the dressing: in a small pan boil the water, sugar and vanilla pod together for about 5 minutes until the liquid is slightly syrupy. Remove the pan from the heat and carefully take out the vanilla pod. (This can be rinsed, dried and used in another recipe – they are far too expensive to waste!)
3. Whisk in the mustard, white wine vinegar and egg yolks, followed by the olive oil, half the chilli and the chives. Cover the pan and keep it warm.
4. Put the noodles in a mixing bowl, pour boiling water over them and leave for 2–3 minutes. This is all the cooking they need.
5. Heat the olive oil in the frying pan and sauté the mango, chilli and mangetout.
6. Drain the noodles and add them to the mangetout mixture.
7. Arrange the noodles on a serving dish and lay the poached chicken on top. Drizzle over the tangy chilli and chive dressing.

1.2 L/2 pt chicken stock (see page 110)

4 x 175 g/6 oz chicken breasts, skinned and boned

For the dressing

4 tablespoons water

4 tablespoons sugar

1 vanilla pod, cut in half lengthways

1 tablespoon Dijon mustard

2 tablespoons white wine vinegar

2 egg yolks

2 tablespoons olive oil

1 fresh red chilli, seeded and finely chopped

1 tablespoon chopped fresh chives

For the noodles

350 g/12 oz angel-hair noodles

1 tablespoon olive oil

1 mango, skinned, flesh cut into small chunks

1 fresh green chilli, seeded and finely chopped

115 g/4 oz mangetout, topped, tailed and shredded

Poached Chicken with a Port Wine Sauce

SERVES 4

For the poached chicken

600 ml/1 pt chicken stock (see page 110)

few sprigs fresh rosemary and thyme

4 x 175 g/6 oz chicken breasts, skinned and boned

2 cucumbers, peeled

25 g/1 oz butter

salt and freshly ground black pepper

15 g/½ oz chives, chopped

For the port wine sauce

4 tablespoons red port

4 tablespoons balsamic vinegar

1 tablespoon whipping cream

150 g/5 oz butter, diced and chilled

We tend to eat cucumber raw, in salads, but here it's cooked and it's absolutely delicious. Try it!

1. Pour the stock into a medium-size pan and bring it to a simmer. Put in the rosemary and thyme, then the chicken breasts, bring back to a gentle simmer and cook for about 10 minutes or until the chicken is tender. Drain the breasts, put them on a plate, cover and keep them warm.

2. Halve the cucumbers lengthways and use a teaspoon to remove the seeds. Cut them across into slices about 5 mm/¼ in thick.

3. Heat the butter in a frying pan and sauté the cucumber for 3–4 minutes, or until it is just tender but still with plenty of bite. Season, and scatter with the chives. Take the pan off the heat and keep it warm.

4. In a small saucepan boil together the port and the balsamic vinegar until about 1 tablespoon of liquid remains. Add the cream and bring back to the boil. Then turn the heat down low and whisk in the butter slowly, piece by piece. Don't let the sauce boil at this stage or it will curdle.

5. To serve, place the sautéed cucumber in the centre of the warmed plates and put a piece of chicken on top. Spoon the port wine sauce around the edge and serve it hot with plain potatoes or pasta.

Nutter's Oriental Bird

SERVES 4

Sometimes our traditional roast chicken can taste rather bland. Try this and you're in for a treat – I'll eat my waistcoat if you go back to your boring roast bird. The chicken is basted with a combination of Oriental ingredients while it is roasting, which gives it a rich, brown, honey-glazed skin and succulent, mildly spiced flesh. Sensational, served hot or cold – and the juices make a fantastic gravy. Wow!

1. Pre-heat the oven to 180°C/350°F/Gas 4/fan oven 160°C.
2. Discard any supermarket string on the bird then remove the giblets, if any, and the internal fat from the parson's nose end. Put the garlic inside the chicken, with a good seasoning of salt and freshly ground black pepper, then sit it in a roasting tin. Don't worry about trussing the chicken, but its appearance will be improved if you tie the legs together.
3. If you have one of those nifty electric spice blenders whizz the marinade ingredients in it; otherwise, just mix them together. Pour the marinade over the bird, and put 150 ml/¼ pt water into the base of the tin, *not* over the chicken.
4. Put it in the oven to roast for 1½ hours and baste it every 20 minutes. If the skin starts to colour too quickly before the bird is ready, cover it loosely with some foil. Check that it is cooked thoroughly by pricking the thickest part of the leg, next to the body. The juices should run clear.
5. Drain the bird, tipping all the juices from the cavity back into the roasting tin, then transfer it to a serving dish. Cover and keep warm.
6. Skim the fat from the juice in the tin, reheat and mash into it any whole garlic cloves that might have fallen out of the chicken. Season to taste and serve with the chicken.
7. A nice accompaniment to this dish is mangetout tossed in butter with chopped ginger, served slightly crunchy. Transform those roast potatoes by adding lots of garlic and sprinkling them with ½ teaspoon of five-spice powder while they are cooking.

2.75 kg/about 4½ lb oven-ready chicken
5 large cloves garlic, peeled
salt and freshly ground black pepper

For the marinade
3 tablespoons clear honey
1 tablespoon light soy sauce
1 tablespoon Worcestershire sauce
1 tablespoon peeled and grated fresh ginger
2 cloves garlic, peeled and finely chopped
1 teaspoon mild paprika
1 teaspoon five-spice powder
juice of ½ lemon
1 tablespoon grainy mustard

Chicken with Coconut Curried Cous-cous

SERVES 4

For the chicken

16 rashers smoked streaky
    bacon, rinded
4 x 175 g/6 oz chicken breasts,
    skinned and boned
small bunch coriander
splash of vegetable oil

For the cous-cous

400 g/14 oz cous-cous
600 ml/1 pt chicken stock (see
    page 110), simmering
1 medium onion, 1 clove garlic,
    1 carrot: all peeled and finely
    chopped
1 leek, white part only, finely
    chopped
2 teaspoons medium curry
    powder
50 g/2 oz butter
salt and freshly ground black
    pepper

For the sauce

1 tablespoon olive oil
1 clove garlic and 1 medium
    onion, peeled and finely
    chopped
1 teaspoon mild paprika
1 teaspoon turmeric
2 teaspoons curry powder
1 teaspoon chilli powder
1 x 400 ml/14 fl oz can coconut
    milk

Transform that 'poultry' piece of chicken with this easy, spicy Indian/Moroccan dish. The spices are Indian, but cous-cous, or semolina, is common in North Africa. It is also great in vegetarian cookery, and I think it is the best instant food ever. Most supermarkets stock it.

1. Pre-heat the oven to 200°C/400°F/Gas 6/fan oven 180°C.
2. Lay four rashers of bacon horizontally, almost overlapping, on a chopping board. Place a chicken breast vertically over the bacon, with about four coriander leaves on it. Wrap the bacon strips alternately around the chicken to make a neat parcel. Repeat with the remaining chicken.
3. Heat a little oil in a hot frying pan. Fry the chicken parcels quickly over a fairly high heat until golden brown on both sides, then transfer them to a baking tray and put it in the oven for about 10 minutes to finish cooking.
4. For the cous-cous, pour the grains into a heat-proof mixing bowl. Have the chicken stock simmering, and add to it the chopped onion, garlic, carrot, leek and curry powder. Boil for about 2 minutes then pour over the cous-cous. Cover it and leave it to stand for 5 minutes.
5. To make the sauce, heat the olive oil in a small pan and fry the garlic and onion in it until softened and golden. Add the paprika, turmeric, curry powder and chilli powder, and cook for 1 minute. Now pour in the coconut milk, bring to a simmer, then remove the pan from the heat. Pour the contents of the pan into a food processor and blend until smooth.
6. Use a large fork to stir the soaked cous-cous, add the butter, taste and correct the seasoning.
7. To serve, pile the cous-cous on to hot serving plates, put a chicken breast on top of each and pour around the coconut and curry sauce.

64

Dazzling Duck Breast with a Honey and Mustard Glaze

SERVES 2

If you are out to impress a lover, this dish will do it. It's a stunner of a dish – I think I may have said that once before!

1. Get the garnish out of the way first. You could dazzle and use a Salfrino scoop to make the carrot into little balls, but don't panic if you don't have one. Grab a potato peeler and cut long carrot ribbons. Put them in a small pan with the butter and sugar, cover and put on one side, ready to cook.
2. Cut the leek into 7.5 cm/3 in lengths. Split the pieces in half lengthways. One at a time, open the halves and press them flat on the work surface. Now shred them into very thin strips, as fine as you can cut them. Heat the oil to 160°C/325°F in a deep pan and fry them until they are crisp and golden brown. Drain on kitchen paper and keep warm.
3. Put a frying pan on to heat. Meanwhile, remove sufficient fat from the duck so that the meat is covered with only a thin layer.
4. Combine the paprika, five-spice powder and curry powder, and coat the duck breast with it.
5. Place the duck, skinned side down, in the hot pan. (There is no need for any fat, as what remains on the duck will render down and be sufficient to cook it.) Leave it to cook over a low to moderate heat for 10–12 minutes, turning every so often so that it becomes crisp on the outside but remains pink in the centre.
6. Put the pan containing the carrots over a low heat to cook.
7. When the duck is cooked to your liking, remove it to a plate. Add the honey and mustard to the pan. Heat gently, stirring for 1 minute, then return the duck to the pan and turn so that it becomes covered in the glaze. Put it back on the plate and keep warm.

For the garnish

2 carrots, peeled
25 g/1 oz butter
1 tablespoon caster sugar
1 leek, trimmed and washed
vegetable oil, for deep-frying

For the duck and sauce

1 x 225 g/8 oz duck breast, Barbary if possible, skin removed
1 teaspoon mild paprika
1 teaspoon five-spice powder
1 teaspoon medium curry powder
2 tablespoons honey
1 tablespoon mustard
2 tablespoons brandy
2 tablespoons red wine
4 tablespoons beef stock
150 ml/¼ pt whipping cream
salt and freshly ground black pepper

For the stir-fry

115 g/4 oz mangetout, topped, tailed and cut in half lengthways
1 tablespoon olive oil
1 tablespoon peeled and finely chopped fresh ginger

8. Add the brandy and red wine to the pan and boil to reduce by half. Then add the beef stock and boil until reduced by half again.

9. Finally add the cream and season to taste. Cover and keep warm.

10. Sauté the mangetout in a hot pan with the olive oil and ginger for about 1 minute.

11. Slice the duck on a clean chopping board and quickly grill it if it needs a little extra cooking.

12. Arrange the mangetout in the middle of each plate in a small pile. Fan the sliced duck around it. Drizzle the sauce around and garnish with the deep-fried leek on top and the carrot round the edge.

Poached Chicken Breast with Knockout Noodles

Dazzling Duck Breast with a Honey and Mustard Glaze

Char-grilled Duck Legs with Barbecued Potatoes and Spicy Chorizo Sausage

SERVES 4

A must for the perfect barbecue. The duck legs are coloured quickly over the flames, wrapped in tin foil with a delicious honey and orange marinade and left to cook slowly until they are tender. Serve with char-grilled potatoes and sausages. I dollop sour cream and chives on top — but, then, I'm slim enough to get away with it!

olive oil

4 x 175 g/6 oz duck legs, or
 1 duckling, quartered

salt and freshly ground black
 pepper

For the marinade

4 tablespoons clear honey

grated zest of 1 orange

1 teaspoon ground cumin

1 tablespoon Dijon mustard

1 clove garlic, peeled and finely
 chopped

1 tablespoon dark soy sauce

1 large baking potato, skin left
 on

115 g/4 oz spicy chorizo
 sausage, skinned

1. Have your barbecue coals really hot or, if the weather isn't up to much, heat a char-grill pan. Also, if you are not using a barbecue, pre-heat the oven to 160°C/325°F/Gas 3/fan oven 140°C.
2. Drizzle a little olive oil over the duck legs, just to stop them sticking, then season them with salt and freshly ground black pepper. Place them on the hottest part of the barbecue, or on the char-grill pan, and cook just until they are browned.
3. While the duck is browning, mix the marinade ingredients together in a bowl. Have ready four squares of foil, large enough to enclose each duck leg. Sit one leg joint on each square, spoon over some of the marinade, and fold the foil into a neat parcel to seal in the juices. Replace the parcels on a cooler barbecue, or put them on a baking tray in the oven for 40 minutes.
4. Now cut the potato into 1cm/½in thick slices and toss them in a little oil and seasoning. Have ready a char-grill pan, wipe it clean, and heat it over the barbecue, or on the stove, then cook the potato slices until they have softened and coloured on both sides.
5. Slice the chorizo thinly at an angle to give oval slices and scatter it around the potatoes. It needs only to heat through as it will toughen if overcooked.
6. After the cooking time is complete, carefully open one

parcel without releasing the juice and test the duck leg with the point of a knife to see if the meat parts easily from the bone. If not, re-seal and cook for a further 10 minutes. When the duck is ready, open each parcel on a warmed plate so that you don't lose any of the juice. Serve with the barbecued potatoes and chorizo sausage.

Medallions of Pork with a Mushroom Risotto

SERVES 4

25 g/1 oz butter

4 x 175 g/6 oz pork fillets, trimmed of fat and sinew

For the mushroom risotto

25 g/1 oz butter

1 medium onion, peeled and finely chopped

1 clove garlic, peeled and finely chopped

175 g/6 oz Arborio rice

2 tablespoons dry white wine

600 ml/1 pt chicken stock (see page 110), simmering

115 g/4 oz button mushrooms, chopped

salt and freshly ground black pepper

about 50 g/2 oz freshly grated Parmesan

For the sauce

15 g/½ oz butter

If pork is not your cup of tea, don't worry: substitute chicken. The combination of the creamy mushroom risotto with freshly grated Parmesan is so good it could be eaten on its own.

1. For the pork, heat the butter in a frying pan until it is nut brown. Then put in the pork fillets and brown them evenly over a moderate heat until the meat is just cooked. Remove them to a plate, cover and keep warm.
2. For the risotto, heat the butter in the same frying pan and cook the onion and garlic until they have softened and lightly coloured, about 8 minutes.
3. Add the rice and cook, stirring, for 1 minute. Pour in the wine and let it bubble until it has almost evaporated. Now start adding the simmering stock, a ladleful at a time. Add sufficient so that the pan can be tilted without the rice sticking, and leave it to cook, stirring frequently, until the rice has absorbed most of the stock before you add more. After 10 minutes add the mushrooms. Continue to add more stock as required until the rice is just cooked and creamy. Season before serving.
4. While the rice is cooking, make the sauce. In a medium-size pan heat the butter, stir in the onion and garlic, then cover and cook for about 5 minutes, or until they have softened but not coloured.

5. Pour in the wine and boil to reduce it by half. Add the chicken stock and reduce by half again. Now put in the cream and simmer gently until it has reduced to give a light sauce consistency. Add the chopped chives and season to taste.
6. To serve, spoon the risotto on to warmed plates. Slice the pork fairly thickly and arrange it on the risotto. Pour the sauce round it and scatter over the grated Parmesan.

1 small onion and 1 clove
   garlic, peeled and finely
   chopped
4 tablespoons dry white wine
4 tablespoons chicken stock
300 ml/½ pt whipping cream
1 tablespoon chopped fresh
   chives
salt and freshly ground black
   pepper

Pork Pieces with Melting Stilton and Chive Fondue

SERVES 4

Fondue was a favourite of mine while I was working in the French Alps, but it did get a bit boring just dipping bread into melted cheese. So I have transformed it into a different and more substantial dish.

1. Heat the butter in a frying pan until it is nut brown. Evenly brown the pork fillets over a moderately high heat for about 5 minutes, turning them occasionally. Lower the heat and continue to cook gently for a further 8–10 minutes.
2. Meanwhile, bring the white wine and garlic to a boil in a medium-sized pan. Remove it from the heat and stir in the cheeses. Replace it over a low heat and cook, stirring frequently, until the cheese has melted.
3. In a small bowl blend the cornflour with 1 tablespoon of water, then stir it into the cheese mixture, followed by the chives and lots of black pepper. Continue to heat gently, not allowing the mixture to boil or the cheese will go hard and stringy.
4. Cook the tagliatelle in plenty of boiling salted water until it is *al dente*. This usually takes only 4–5 minutes, but it varies according to brand, and whether the pasta is fresh or dried. Drain it and toss it with butter, and season to taste.

25 g/1 oz butter
4 x 175 g/6 oz pork fillets,
   trimmed of fat and sinew

For the fondue
175 ml/6 fl oz dry white wine
1 clove garlic, peeled and finely
   chopped
115 g/4 oz Gruyère, diced
115 g/4 oz Emmental, diced
115 g/4 oz Stilton, diced
2 teaspoons cornflour
1 tablespoon chopped fresh
   chives
freshly ground black pepper

To serve
350 g/12 oz fresh *or* dried
   tagliatelle
50 g/2 oz butter

5. Stir the cheese mixture, which should now have combined to form a sauce. Remove the pan from the heat.

6. Quickly slice the cooked pork. Arrange a portion of pasta in the centre of each serving plate and the pork slices on top. Pour the cheese fondue over the pork and serve immediately.

Thai-style Pork Medallions

SERVES 4

4 x 175 g/6 oz pork fillets, fat and sinew removed

2 cloves garlic, chopped

1 stem fresh lemon grass, trimmed to 10–12 cm/4–5 in, finely chopped

1 red chilli, seeded and finely chopped

1 green chilli, seeded and finely chopped

1 tablespoon peeled and finely chopped fresh ginger

2 tablespoons light soy sauce

2 tablespoons olive oil

For the cous-cous

600 ml/1 pt chicken stock (see page 110)

1 clove garlic, peeled and finely chopped

1 medium onion, peeled and finely chopped

1 tablespoon peeled and finely chopped fresh ginger

Do try to find the Thai ingredients for this dish — if you're desperate, ordinary cream and a squeeze of lemon juice will work, but it is not the same as the authentic Thai taste you get from lemon grass and coconut milk. And before anyone writes in, I know cous-cous is not Thai, but in this recipe it does complement the pork!

1. Put the pork fillets in a dish. Combine the garlic, lemon grass, chillies, ginger and soy, then spread the mixture over the pork fillets. Cover and leave in a cool place to marinate for at least 2 hours.

2. Heat the olive oil in a frying pan. Scrape off and save all the marinade that coated the pork. Dry the meat on kitchen paper and fry it in the oil until it is golden brown all over. Reduce the heat to low and continue to fry, turning occasionally until the pork is cooked through, about 10–12 minutes.

3. Meanwhile, for the cous-cous, pour the chicken stock into a small pan, add the garlic, onion and ginger and bring to the boil. Have the cous-cous ready in a heat-proof bowl. Taste and season the stock then pour it on to the cous-cous, cover and leave it to stand for about 5 minutes. Chop and add the spring onions and small dabs of butter. Stir through, cover again and keep it warm.

4. Remove the cooked pork from the pan, wrap it in foil and keep warm.

5. For the sauce, pour the white wine into the pork pan and heat it, stirring and scraping the residue from the base. Now add the coconut milk, bring it to a simmer, add the coriander and season to taste.

6. Serve a bed of cous-cous on the warmed serving plates. Slice each pork fillet and arrange the slices on the grains. Finally, spoon a generous quantity of sauce over the meat.

225 g/8 oz medium cous-cous

salt and freshly ground black pepper

I bunch spring onions, base and tops trimmed, leaving 7.5 cm/3 in green

25 g/I oz butter

For the sauce

200 ml/7 fl oz white wine

I x 400 ml can coconut milk

I tablespoon chopped coriander leaves

Lamb Cutlets with Caramelized Roast Vegetables

SERVES 4

You'll think you're in the Mediterranean with this dish. The flavours and textures must be tasted to be believed and the colours are out of this world!

1. Place the lamb cutlets in a shallow dish and sprinkle with the olive oil, garlic and herbs. Turn them in the mixture then cover and leave in a cool place for approximately 2 hours for the flavour to infuse.

2. Pre-heat the oven to 220°C/425°F/Gas 7/fan oven 200°C.

3. Cut the aubergine, red and yellow peppers into neat, small, chip shapes. Mix them with the shallots, new potatoes and olive oil.

4. Place them in a roasting tray large enough to take them in a single layer, and put them in the oven to roast for about 15 minutes.

5. Add the courgette to the vegetables in the roasting tray with the garlic and honey. Stir to mix in the honey,

For the lamb

12 lamb cutlets, trimmed of fat

6–8 tablespoons olive oil

I clove garlic, peeled and coarsely chopped

bunch of mixed fresh herbs (basil, thyme, rosemary), coarsely chopped

For the roast vegetables

I aubergine

I red pepper, seeded

I yellow pepper, seeded

12 shallots, peeled and halved

12 new potatoes, half-cooked and halved

4 tablespoons olive oil

1 courgette, sliced

2 cloves garlic, peeled and
  chopped

1 tablespoon honey

salt and freshly ground black
  pepper

4 basil leaves, shredded

season generously and return them to the oven for approximately 5 minutes more to give the vegetables time to caramelize.

6. Remove the cutlets from the marinade and season well. Heat an empty frying pan over a moderate heat for 2–3 minutes to make sure the cutlets are seared the instant they come into contact with it. Fry them until they are golden brown.

7. Remove the vegetables from the oven and scatter the shredded basil over them. Serve alongside the cooked cutlets.

Medallions of Lamb with Creamy Cabbage

SERVES 4

Cabbage may not be everyone's favourite vegetable as it is often overcooked and stewed. Mine is stir-fried and steamed in the same pan seconds later, which brings out all its lovely flavours yet leaves it crisp and nutritious.

splash of olive oil

4 x 175 g/6 oz lamb fillets,
  trimmed

For the creamy cabbage

1 tablespoon olive oil

4 rashers smoked streaky
  bacon, rinded and chopped

1 large onion, peeled and
  chopped

1 clove garlic, peeled and
  chopped

1 carrot, peeled and chopped

½ Savoy cabbage, finely
  shredded

200 ml/7 fl oz chicken stock
  (see page 110)

200 ml/7 fl oz whipping cream

salt and freshly ground pepper

1. Heat the splash of olive oil in a frying pan and brown the meat over a fairly high heat. Now reduce the heat and continue cooking until the meat is done to your liking. Remove to a plate; cover and keep warm.

2. Add the tablespoon of olive oil to the frying pan, and cook the chopped bacon until it is golden brown.

3. Add the onion, garlic and carrot and continue cooking for a couple of minutes.

4. Put in the cabbage and cook it over a high heat for about a minute. Then add the stock – it will give off a lot of steam – and stir thoroughly to dislodge the sediments from the bottom of the pan.

5. Finally add the cream, briefly reheat and season to taste.

6. Carve the lamb in thick oblique slices and serve it with the creamy cabbage.

Peppered Steak with Mushroom Mash

SERVES 4

The nation's favourite. This recipe suggests fillet steak but you could use sirloin or rump – it really depends on your budget or what you prefer. Whatever you use, though, the sauce and the accompanying mushroom mash are simply knockout.

1. Start with the mushroom mash. Heat the butter in a medium-size pan and fry the onion and garlic over a moderate heat for about 5 minutes, or until they have softened and are golden.
2. Add the mushrooms, stir and cook for 1 minute, then put in the potatoes – crush them with a fork until they are broken up.
3. Stir in the parsley, mustard and cream. Season to taste then cover and keep warm until you are ready to serve.
4. Press the crushed peppercorns on to the steak. Heat the butter in a frying pan until it is nut brown when it will be hot enough to cook the steaks – anything less means that the meat will stew. Fry the steaks until they are done to your liking, rare or medium. (My advice is to start checking after they have been on for about 4 minutes in total, and to undercook them slightly anyway, to allow for the time they will keep warm while you make the sauce and dish up.) Remove them from the pan, cover and keep warm.
5. Now make the sauce. Add the onion and garlic to the fat remaining in the pan and cook for about 3 minutes until they have softened. Pour in the brandy and wine and boil until the liquid has reduced by half.
6. Now add the beef stock and boil again until it has reduced by half. Stir in the cream, chives and pink peppercorns, then season to taste.
7. Arrange the steaks and the mash on the plates and, lastly, spoon the sauce over the meat

For the mushroom mash
25 g/1 oz butter
1 small onion, peeled and finely chopped
1 clove garlic, peeled and finely chopped
115 g/4 oz mushrooms, wiped and chopped
2 large potatoes, peeled and freshly boiled
2 tablespoons chopped fresh parsley
1 teaspoon wholegrain mustard
4 tablespoons whipping cream
salt and freshly ground pepper

For the peppered steak
4 x 175 g/6 oz fillet steaks
1 tablespoon crushed black peppercorns
25 g/1 oz butter

For the sauce
1 small onion and 1 clove garlic, peeled and finely chopped
50 ml//2 fl oz brandy
125 ml/4 fl oz red wine
125 ml/4 fl oz beef stock
50 ml/2 fl oz whipping cream
1 tablespoon chopped fresh chives
½ tablespoon pink peppercorns

Puddings

Banoffee Treasure Chest with Hazelnut Fudge Sauce

Black and White Minstrel Cheesecake

Chilled Delicate Chocolate Desserts

Chocolate and Banana Timbale with a Liquid Chocolate Centre

Choux Swans on a Strawberry Lake

Hot Chocolate Pizza with Strawberry Milkshake Sauce

Custard Cream Ice-cream

Orange Soufflé Omelette

Frozen Passion Fruit and Lemon Mousse

Pancakes with Nutter's Favourite Fillings

Peach and Almond Tart

Pineapple Baked Alaska

Strawberry Crème Brûlée

Tiramisu Profiteroles

Mille-feuille of Alcoholic Fruits

Banoffee Treasure Chest with Hazelnut Fudge Sauce

SERVES 4

Indulge yourself in this version of a Banoffee Pie. Hot slices of banana rest on a bed of rum-flavoured mashed bananas, slipped between layers of puff pastry. Drizzle this with a rich toffee-style sauce, and you have a dessert made in heaven.

1. Pre-heat the oven to 180°C/350°F/Gas 4/fan oven 160°C.
2. Roll out the pastry to a rectangle about 30 cm x 10 cm x 5–8 mm/12 in x 4 in x ¼–⅜ in thick. Cut into 4 equal rectangular pieces.
3. Place the rectangles on a baking tray and brush them with beaten egg yolk. Use a cocktail stick or small knife to mark the top with a criss-cross pattern. Bake for 10–15 minutes, or until well risen and golden brown. Remove the pastry from the oven but leave it on the baking tray and don't switch off the oven.
4. Quickly make the banana filling: mash 2 of the bananas with the lemon juice, cream, rum and cinnamon. No need to put in any sugar as the sauce provides enough sweetening.
5. Slice the cooked pastry rectangles in half horizontally. Place a spoonful of the mashed banana mix in the bottom half of each rectangle.
6. Slice the remaining bananas thinly and arrange them neatly on top of the banana filling. Replace the lids and put the pastries back in the oven for 4–5 minutes to warm through.
7. Meanwhile, make the sauce. Put the butter, sugar and syrup in a small pan. Bring it to the boil and simmer for about 3 minutes until the sauce has turned a golden brown. Remove it from the heat and stir in the cream and hazelnuts.
8. Serve the pastries on warmed plates with some of the hazelnut fudge sauce spooned over. It's awesome on its own, or even more wicked served with ice-cream or fresh pouring cream.

For the pastry
250 g/9 oz puff pastry
a little flour for rolling
1 egg yolk, beaten

For the banana filling
4 ripe bananas
juice of ½ small lemon
2 tablespoons whipping cream
1 tablespoon rum
1 teaspoon ground cinnamon

For the sauce
50 g/2 oz butter
115 g/4 oz soft light brown sugar
115 g/4 oz golden syrup
150 ml/¼ pt whipping cream
1 tablespoon chopped hazelnuts

Black and White Minstrel Cheesecake

MAKES 10

For the dark chocolate layer

I leaf gelatine

I egg yolk

25g/I oz caster sugar

I tablespoon dark rum

50 g/2 oz plain chocolate,
   melted in a small bowl over
   a saucepan of boiling water

110 g/4 oz full fat cream
   cheese

80 ml/2½ fl oz whipping cream

I egg white

10 Galaxy Minstrel chocolates,
   crushed

For the white chocolate layer

I leaf gelatine

I egg yolk

25g/I oz caster sugar

I tablespoon white rum

50 g/2 oz white chocolate,
   melted as above

110 g/4 oz full fat cream
   cheese

80ml/2½ fl oz whipping cream

I egg white

For the base

100 g/4 oz digestive biscuits,
   crushed

50 g/2 oz butter, melted

50 g/2 oz Demerara sugar

Both dark and white chocolate is used in this lovely version of the cheesecake. The quantities given here will make 10 cheesecakes, because it is too much effort to halve them – when did you last try to cut an egg yolk in half? What I suggest is that you use this as a party dish, or when four of your most chocoholic friends come round. But it is too good to ignore. The smoothness of the white chocolate mixture is in complete contrast to the crisp, crunchy dark chocolate mixture. If you can't get hold of Minstrels, replace them with chopped chocolate, but you will lose the distinctive crisp texture. Incidentally, I prefer to use leaf gelatine but if you can't find it, buy gelatine granules. Substitute ½ teaspoon of granules for each leaf of gelatine, dissolved completely in 2 tablespoons of boiling water.

1. Have ready ten 150 ml/¼ pt ramekins, lightly greased, on a baking tray.
2. To make the dark cheesecake layer, start by breaking the gelatine into several small pieces and put it in a small bowl with 2 tablespoons of cold water. Leave it to soften.
3. Put the egg yolk and half the sugar in a medium-size, heat-proof bowl over a pan of water at just below boiling point. Whisk for I minute, then add the rum and continue to whisk for another minute until the mixture becomes fluffy.
4. Drain the softened gelatine and add it to the egg mixture. Continue whisking until the gelatine has dissolved.
5. Remove the bowl and pan from the heat and stir in the plain chocolate – you may find the mixture will go quite firm at this point but don't worry, it will be perfect in the end! Put in the cream cheese and beat until the mixture is smooth.
6. Whisk the cream until it has thickened a little, then gently fold it into the chocolate.
7. In a clean bowl whisk together the egg white and the remaining sugar until the mixture is light and fluffy. Fold

very gently into the chocolate along with the crushed Minstrels until you have a uniform mix.

8. Divide this equally between the ramekin dishes then chill in the fridge.
9. To make the white cheesecake layer, repeat the process above, replacing the dark chocolate with the white chocolate, the dark rum with the white rum and omitting the Minstrels. Spoon the mixture into the ramekins, on top of the dark layer, and chill again.
10. Now make the base. Mix the biscuits with the butter and sugar, then gently press the crumbs on top of the white cheesecake in the ramekins and replace in the fridge for a minimum of 2 hours to finish setting.
11. When you are ready to serve, turn out the cheesecakes by dipping the ramekins in hot water for a few seconds, then inverting them on to serving plates. Serve with pouring cream and decorate with seasonal fruits.

Note: For a special occasion serve with Black and White Biscuits (see page 97).

Chilled Delicate Chocolate Desserts

MAKES 6

This absolutely delicious dessert is a cross between a crème caramel and chocolate blancmange. It is smooth, creamy, chocolaty and just melts in the mouth.

1 tablespoon water
100 g/4 oz caster sugar
375 ml/13 fl oz milk
150 ml/¼ pt whipping cream
1 teaspoon vanilla extract
1 teaspoon coffee granules
100 g/4 oz plain chocolate, broken into squares
1 egg
3 egg yolks

1. Pre-heat the oven to 180°C/350°F/Gas 4/fan oven 160°C.
2. In a saucepan boil the water and sugar until it is the colour of golden syrup. Add the milk, cream, vanilla, coffee and chocolate, and bring it to a simmer.
3. Place the egg and yolks in a bowl, whisk them lightly and then pour the chocolate mixture on to them, whisking as you pour to prevent the eggs curdling.

To decorate
6 strawberries, sliced
6 teaspoons coffee liqueur
150 ml/¼ pt whipping cream
1 drop vanilla extract
25 g/1 oz icing sugar, sifted
25 g/1 oz white chocolate,
  grated

4. Pour the chocolate mixture into 6 x 150 ml/¼ pt ramekin dishes and put them in a roasting tin. Pour sufficient tap-hot water into the tin to come three-quarters of the way up the ramekins. (This creates a hot-water bath, which cooks the chocolate mixture gently while it is in the oven.)

5. Cover the tin with foil then transfer it to the oven for 25 minutes. The mixture should be set and very slightly puffed up when it is ready. Remove the tin from the oven, take the ramekins out of the water and leave to cool.

6. Once the chocolate desserts are cool, place them in the fridge to chill for at least 1 hour.

7. When you are ready to serve, lay a few slices of strawberry on top of each chocolate dessert, and drizzle over about a teaspoon of coffee liqueur.

8. Whisk the cream with the vanilla and the icing sugar until it has thickened, then place a generous teaspoonful of it on top of the strawberries. Scatter the white chocolate over the top.

Chocolate and Banana Timbale with a Liquid Chocolate Centre

MAKES 5

This recipe takes time to prepare and involves three stages. Don't be put off, because the end is seriously sensational!

1. Pre-heat the oven to 160°C/325°F/Gas 3/fan oven 140°C.

2. Grease and line the base and sides of a 15 cm/6 in cake tin with greaseproof paper or baking parchment. Grease the paper.

3. For stage 1: beat the butter and both types of sugar thoroughly together until the mixture is pale and fluffy. Beat in the egg, then fold in the banana and lemon juice.

4. Sift the flour and baking powder into the bowl and fold it into the mixture. Spoon it into the prepared tin then put it into the oven to bake for about 40 minutes, or until the

For stage 1, the banana cake
50 g/2 oz butter
50 g/2 oz caster sugar
25 g/1 oz soft light brown sugar
1 egg
1 ripe banana, mashed with a
  fork
1 teaspoon lemon juice
100 g/4 oz plain flour
½ teaspoon baking powder

cake is risen, firm in the centre and shows signs of shrinking away from the sides of the tin. Leave it to cool for a few minutes, then turn it out on to a wire rack and leave it to finish cooling. Raise the oven temperature to 180°C/350°F/Gas 4/fan oven 160°C.

5. For stage 2: combine the eggs, egg yolk and brown sugar together in a small bowl and beat until they are thoroughly mixed.

6. Then, in a medium-size pan, combine the cream, milk, chocolate and butter, bring it to the boil, stirring occasionally, and, whisking all the time, pour it directly on to the egg mixture. Leave the chocolate custard to stand for a few minutes.

7. Cut the cooled cake into 2-cm/¾-in dice and put them into a bowl. Pour the chocolate custard over the cake, cover the bowl with cling-film and leave it for about 20 minutes to allow the custard to soak into the cake.

8. For stage 3: while the cake is soaking up the sauce, very gently warm the cream and chocolate until the mixture has melted and is smooth. Remove it from the heat and stir in the butter. When that has melted stir in the rum, and leave the chocolate cream to cool.

9. Now to assemble the puddings – you're into the home straight! Grease 5 x 150 ml/¼ pint ramekins with butter. Half-fill each with the chocolate-custard-soaked cake.

10. Take a teaspoon of the chocolate cream and place a blob in the centre of each ramekin. Divide the remaining chocolate-custard-cake mix between the ramekins, making sure that the cream is fully enclosed in the centre of the pudding.

11. Bake for 10 minutes or until the puddings are set. Don't overcook them or they will rise and the centre will bubble out like a miniature volcano!

12. Serve the puddings in the ramekins, or carefully loosen the sides with a knife and turn them out on to serving plates. Decorate with banana slices and mint, and I can thoroughly recommend you serve a vanilla or clotted cream ice-cream with the timbales.

For stage 2, the chocolate custard

2 eggs

I egg yolk

50 g/2 oz soft light brown sugar

50 ml/2 fl oz whipping cream

225 ml/8 fl oz milk

115 g/4 oz plain chocolate, broken into sections

25 g/1 oz butter

For stage 3, the chocolate cream

I tablespoon cream

75 g/3 oz plain chocolate, broken into sections

15 g/½ oz butter

I tablespoon rum

To decorate

banana slices

sprigs of fresh mint

ice-cream

Choux Swans on a Strawberry Lake

MAKES 10 swans

1 quantity Choux Pastry (see
    page 110)

For the filling
300 ml/½ pt whipping cream
50 g/2 oz icing sugar, sifted
1 teaspoon vanilla extract

For the strawberry lake
175 g/6 oz fresh, hulled
    strawberries
about 25 g/1 oz icing sugar

To decorate
1 small carton plain yoghurt
additional icing sugar
a few fresh mint leaves
some small, fresh, whole
    strawberries

There is no mystery to making choux pastry – so come on! Set to and try out this idea. The result is a delight and not just for children.

1. Pre-heat the oven to 180°C/350°F/Gas 4/fan oven 160°C.
2. Make up the choux pastry according to the recipe. Fit a 1-cm/½-in plain piping nozzle into a large piping bag. Fill the bag with the choux paste.
3. Have ready 2 greased and floured baking trays. Pipe out 10 of each of the shapes outlined below, putting 'heads' on one tray, 'bodies' on the other: the smaller heads will need less cooking time than the bodies. Clean the piping bag.
4. Bake the heads for 15–20 minutes, and the bodies for about 30 minutes. Make sure the pastries are well cooked – the only secret to choux pastry is baking it for long enough to cook through and dry out in the centre. Leave the shapes to cool in a single layer on a wire rack.
5. For the filling, whisk together the cream, icing sugar and vanilla until it forms quite firm peaks, then refrigerate it until you are ready to use it.
6. Take each choux body and slice it in half horizontally. Take the top slice and cut it in half lengthways – to form wings. Fit a rosette nozzle in the piping bag and pipe cream rosettes into the bottom half of the body. Prop the head

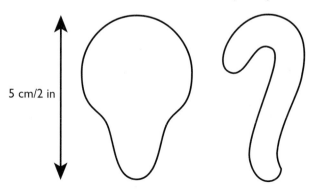

5 cm/2 in

Lamb Cutlets with Caramelized Roast Vegetables

Black and White Minstrel Cheesecake with Black and White Biscuits

on the cream at the broader end of the base. Arrange the 2 wings in place so they taper towards the narrow end of the body, with the cream showing between.

7. Make the strawberry lake. Put the strawberries and icing sugar in the food processor and blend until smooth, then pass the mixture through a sieve to remove the seeds. Taste and add more sugar if you like.

8. To assemble the dessert, pour some of the strawberry sauce in a pool on a plate. Beat the yoghurt to make sure it is smooth, then drop a teaspoonful in the centre of the strawberry sauce. Take a cocktail stick and draw lines from the yoghurt into the sauce to suggest ripples. Put a swan in the centre then dust with icing sugar.

9. Decorate with fresh strawberries and mint leaves, then serve.

Hot Chocolate Pizza with Strawberry Milkshake Sauce

MAKES 4

For the base

250 g/9 oz puff pastry

1 jar chocolate and hazelnut spread

250 g/9 oz punnet of strawberries, hulled

For the chocolate topping

140 g/5 oz plain dark chocolate

15 g/½ oz butter

25 g/1 oz shelled pistachio nuts, finely chopped

3 eggs, separated

70 g/2½ oz caster sugar

For the milkshake sauce

150 ml/¼ pt chilled milk

2 scoops strawberry ice-cream

50 g/2 oz white chocolate, shaved into slivers

A sweet pizza – yes, that's right. It's all an illusion: crisp pastry instead of bread, strawberries instead of tomatoes, and shavings of white chocolate to imitate Parmesan.

1. Pre-heat the oven to 190°C/375°F/Gas 5/fan oven 170°C.
2. Roll out the pastry thinly to cover a 33 x 30 cm/13 x 12 in baking tray. Prick it all over with a fork and bake it in a hot oven for 8–10 minutes until it is golden. Leave it to cool.
3. Cut the cooked and cooled pastry into discs of 9.5–10 cm/3¾ in diameter and put them to one side.
4. For the topping, melt the dark chocolate and butter in a heat-proof bowl over a pan of simmering water. Remove the bowl and stir in the chopped nuts and egg yolks.
5. In a large bowl whisk the egg whites then gradually whisk in the sugar until light and fluffy. Fold gently into the chocolate mixture.
6. Cover the pastry circles with some of the chocolate and hazelnut spread. Slice 2 strawberries per pizza thinly and lay them on top of the chocolate spread.
7. Turn down the oven temperature to 180°C/350°F/Gas 4/fan oven 160°C. Place a greased metal ring about 8.5–9 cm/3½ in (an egg poaching/muffin ring is ideal) on top of each pastry disc and fill it with 3–4 tablespoons of the chocolate topping. Lay all the bases on a baking sheet and put them in the oven for 8 minutes. If you prefer a firmer pudding cook for a little longer.
8. While the pizzas are cooking, make the milkshake sauce. Put the milk, ice-cream and remaining strawberries into a blender and process until the mixture is light and fluffy.
9. Take the pizzas from the oven and remove the metal rings. Put each on a plate and pour the milkshake sauce around it. Scatter over some white chocolate shavings and serve straight away.

Custard Cream Ice-cream

MAKES ABOUT 1.4 L/2½ pt

If you're a fan of custard-cream biscuits then this ice-cream is just for you – it's crunchy, custardy and cool.

1. Heat the milk with the vanilla pod to just below boiling point. Cover and leave it to infuse for 10 minutes. Remove the vanilla pod.
2. Mix the yolks and sugar together in a bowl. Then gradually stir in the flour so the mixture forms a paste. Bring the milk back to just below boiling, pour half on to the egg mixture and whisk together.
3. Pour the egg and milk mixture back into the remaining milk in the pan and heat gently, stirring all the time, until the mixture has thickened and the flour has cooked, about 5 minutes.
4. Pour the custard into a bowl and leave it to cool. Dust with icing sugar to prevent a skin forming. You can speed up the process by sitting the base of the bowl in a larger bowl of cold water.
5. When the custard has cooled, stir in the chilled cream.
6. If you are using an ice-cream machine, churn the mixture until it is softly frozen. Scoop the ice-cream into a plastic storage container, sprinkling liberally with the crumbled biscuits as you go. Stir briefly and transfer it quickly to the freezer until it is firm.
7. If you don't have a machine, pour the mixture into a large plastic box and transfer this to the freezer until the ice-cream is softly frozen. Now beat it either in a food processor or with an electric hand whisk. Return the mixture quickly to the freezer and repeat the process once more as soon as the ice-cream has become softly frozen again. This time when you return it to the container, sprinkle it with the biscuits, then freeze until it is firm.
8. Eat it within a couple of days (or the biscuits will lose their crunch), although once you've had a spoonful, it won't last five minutes.

600 ml/1 pt milk
1 vanilla pod, halved
    lengthways
5 egg yolks
120 g/4 oz caster sugar
25 g/1 oz flour
300 ml/½ pt whipping cream,
    chilled
175 g/6 oz custard cream
    biscuits, coarsely crumbled
    by hand

Orange Soufflé Omelette

SERVES 1

For the fruit salad sauce

¼ small pineapple, peeled and
  cored

½ banana, peeled

I orange

125 g/4½ oz strawberries,
  hulled

25 g/I oz butter

I tablespoon orange liqueur

I tablespoon brandy

2 tablespoons cream

For the soufflé omelette

3 eggs, separated

I tablespoon caster sugar

25 g/I oz butter

about I tablespoon icing sugar,
  sifted

Many people panic when they see the word soufflé but don't be put off by the name. I used to hate eating normal omelettes until my mum made me a version of this recipe when I was fourteen – ever since then I've been hooked. Note: The recipe is for one: multiply the ingredients for more, but bear in mind that each omelette must be cooked separately.

1. Pre-heat the grill to medium.
2. Cut the pineapple and banana into chunky pieces and set aside. Using a zester, remove the orange rind and reserve it. Now peel and segment the orange and put it in a bowl with the strawberries.
3. Heat the butter in a frying pan and sauté the pineapple and banana. Add the orange liqueur and the brandy.
4. Add the orange segments, strawberries and any juice, then stir in the cream. Keep the fruit mixture warm while you prepare the omelette.
5. Whisk the egg whites with the caster sugar until they are light and fluffy. Gently fold in the egg yolks and add the reserved orange zest.
6. Heat the butter in an omelette pan or a small frying pan, then pour in the omelette mixture and cook until it is golden brown on the underside. Then place the whole pan under the grill to cook the top. Watch it like a hawk at this stage as it browns surprisingly quickly.
7. When the omelette is golden brown on top, remove it from the grill, fold it in half, put it on a plate and dust with the icing sugar. Pour the fruit salad sauce round and serve immediately with some extra pouring cream.

Frozen Passion Fruit and Lemon Mousse

MAKES 1.4 L/2½ pt, sufficient for 10 x 150 ml/¼ pt ramekins

A delicious, tangy mousse and a great standby dessert whether served in individual ramekins or cut into slices. Just keep it in the freezer until you need it.

150 ml/¼ pt lemon juice (about 6 lemons)

1½ teaspoons gelatine

finely grated zest of 1 lemon

5 passion fruit, halved, flesh scooped out with a teaspoon

3 eggs, separated

115 g/4 oz caster sugar

225 ml/8 fl oz whipping cream at room temperature

1. If you would prefer to serve this dessert in slices, you will need either a plastic freezer box or an old ice-cream tub of 1.4 L/2½ pt capacity, or use 10 x 150 ml/¼ pt ramekins, lined with cling-film.
2. Heat the lemon juice but do not let it boil then pour it on to the gelatine in a bowl and whisk it in with a fork until it is thoroughly mixed. Leave on one side until the gelatine has dissolved and the liquid has cooled.
3. Meanwhile combine the egg yolks and half the sugar in a large bowl. Whisk for 3–4 minutes or until the mixture is light and fluffy, then stir in the cooled lemon juice and gelatine, the lemon zest and the passion fruit pulp. Leave it until it is syrupy and on the point of setting. You can sit the bowl in cold water to speed up the process.
4. Whisk the cream until it forms soft peaks, then fold it into the passion-fruit mixture. Wash the beaters in soapy water and dry them well, so they are ready to use again.
5. Put the egg whites in a large grease-free mixing bowl with the remaining 50 g/2 oz sugar and whisk until the mixture holds soft peaks. Mix one large spoonful of it into the passion-fruit to loosen the mix, then fold in the rest. Pour into your chosen mould(s), and place in the freezer for 2–3 hours until firm.
6. If you have used ramekins, unmould the mousse 30 minutes before serving by tugging at the cling-film. Unmould it from a plastic box by dipping the box in hot water for 10 seconds, inverting it on to a clean board and cutting it into slices. Place the servings on individual plates and decorate with seasonal fruits.

Pancakes with Nutter's Favourite Fillings

MAKES 12–14 pancakes

For the pancakes

115 g/4 oz plain flour, sifted

2 large eggs

300 ml/½ pt milk

2 tablespoons melted butter

butter, for cooking

Why wait until Shrove Tuesday for this most mouth watering of dishes? The pancakes can be served on their own, with lemon and caster sugar – or try my fillings and sauces.

1. Place the flour in a bowl. Break the eggs into a well in the centre and use a whisk to mix them in, gradually working in the surrounding flour. Then start to add the milk, a little at a time, until all of it has been incorporated and the batter is smooth. If it is lumpy, don't worry, just pour it through a sieve to remove the lumps. Or you can put all the pancake ingredients in a food processor and blend until they are smooth.
2. Just before you fry the pancakes, stir in the melted butter.
3. Put a small knob of butter into a medium-size frying pan and heat it until it has turned nut brown.
4. Pour 3 tablespoons of batter into the hot pan and immediately tip it to get the base covered in a nice even layer. After about 1 minute, or when the pancake is golden brown underneath, turn, or toss it! Cook the other side for about 30 seconds and then remove it from the pan.
5. Continue from step 3 until you have used all the batter. Stack the cooked pancakes with squares of greaseproof paper between them to prevent them sticking together.

Now for the fillings. You will need to make the French-style custard first, a lighter, thicker version of our traditional sloppy English custard. Fill the pancakes with it and serve with the Toffee and Banana Sauce. Or flavour the custard with chocolate and use it to fill pancakes served with the Chocolate and Rum Sauce.

French-style Custard

1. Bring the milk to the boil with the vanilla pod then remove it from the heat and leave it to infuse for about 5 minutes.
2. Mix the egg yolks with the caster sugar, add the plain flour and beat until it is thoroughly combined.
3. Remove the vanilla pod, pour half the milk into the egg mixture, then pour it all into the pan of remaining milk. Whisk over a low heat for about 1 minute until the custard has thickened.

600 ml/1 pt milk
1 vanilla pod, split in half
  lengthways
4 egg yolks
115 g/4 oz caster sugar
50 g/2 oz plain flour, sifted

Toffee and Banana Sauce

1. Boil the sugar with the water in a small pan until it turns golden brown.
2. Remove it from the heat and add the cream – with caution: it will splutter a bit. Whisk in the butter.
3. Chop the banana finely and add it to the toffee sauce.
4. Fill the pancakes with French-style custard, spoon over the sauce and serve.

115 g/4 oz caster sugar
2 tablespoons water
6 tablespoons single cream
50 g/2 oz butter
1 banana, peeled

Chocolate and Rum Sauce

1. Mix the 115 g/4 oz chocolate with the warm French-style custard. When it has melted and the custard is smooth, use it to fill the pancakes.
2. Warm the rum, cream, sugar and the 50 g/2 oz chocolate, and stir until it has melted. Pour this over the filled pancakes and serve.

115 g/4 oz plain chocolate,
  broken into squares

For the sauce
6 tablespoons rum
150 ml/¼ pt whipping cream
1 teaspoon sugar
50 g/2 oz plain chocolate,
  broken into squares

Peach and Almond Tart

SERVES 4–6, depending on how big you like your slices!

For the pastry
225 g/8 oz plain flour

115 g/4 oz butter, chilled and cubed

1 egg yolk

3 tablespoons ice-cold water

For the filling
8 tablespoons apricot jam

85 g/3 oz butter, at room temperature

85 g/3 oz caster sugar

2 eggs

85 g/3 oz ground almonds

1 teaspoon almond extract

2 ripe white peaches

What a combination – a moreish warm tart of frangipane topped with slivers of succulent white peaches and served à la mode with Custard Cream Ice-cream (see page 85).

1. Pre-heat the oven to 180°C/350°F/Gas 4/fan oven 160°C and put into it a baking tray to heat.
2. For the quickest pastry in the world, put the flour and butter in a food processor and blitz until the mixture resembles breadcrumbs. Mix the egg yolk with the water, pour it into the food processor and blitz again until the mixture comes together in a ball. It's done in a minute!
3. Roll out the pastry thinly and use it to line a 20 x 4 cm/ 8 x 1½ in flan ring with a removable base.
4. Now for the filling. Spread the pastry base with half of the jam.
5. Beat together the butter and sugar until it is light and fluffy, then beat in the eggs one at a time. Next, stir in the ground almonds and the almond extract.
6. Spread the filling mixture on top of the jam in the pastry base and put the flan tin on top of the baking tray in the oven for 30 minutes, or until the filling is risen and browned.
7. Meanwhile, thinly slice the peaches. As soon as the filling has cooked, remove the tart from the oven and arrange the peach slices on top in a spiral design.
8. Gently warm the remaining jam, then use it to brush the peach slices to give them a nice glaze.
9. Replace the tart in the oven for a further 5 minutes to cook the peaches a little. Serve the tart warm, topped with scoops of the Custard Cream Ice-cream (see page 85).

Pineapple Baked Alaska

SERVES 4

If you keep a sponge in the freezer, this is a simple dessert to knock together for extra guests. The combination of hot meringue and cold ice-cream will wow the kids. Not only does it taste delicious, it looks, or should look, like a stunning pineapple.

You can freeze the cake trimmings and use to make my Quick Rum Truffles on page 103.

1 small ripe pineapple
1 x 18 cm/7 in diameter
  basic sponge (see
  page 109)
2 tablespoons rum
2 egg whites
120 g/4 oz caster sugar
few drops vanilla extract
1 small tub rum and raisin *or*
  vanilla ice-cream

1. Pre-heat the oven to 200°C/400°F/Gas 6/fan oven 180°C.
2. Prepare the pineapple by removing the skin and core – reserve the leaves. Cut the flesh into small chunks.
3. Cut the round sponge into an oval and put it on an attractive oval ovenproof serving plate. Lay some of the pineapple chunks on the sponge in an even layer, then pour on the rum.
4. Put the egg whites in a bowl and whisk until they are fluffy. Slowly whisk in the sugar and add the vanilla. Continue whisking until the meringue is firm enough to form stiff peaks.
5. Place four to five scoops of ice-cream on top of the pineapple chunks.
6. Now, you can either put the meringue into a piping bag fitted with a 1 cm/½ in nozzle and pipe little blobs all over the dessert to resemble the skin of a pineapple, or, if you prefer, you can spread the meringue all over the sponge and ice-cream and use a palette knife to form spikes. It is most important that all the ice-cream is covered with the meringue, or it will melt in the oven.
7. Put it in the oven for 3–4 minutes until it is golden brown.
8. Remove the Baked Alaska from the oven, decorate it with the remaining pineapple chunks around the edge and restore the leaves to the end of your mock pineapple. Serve straight away.

Strawberry Crème Brûlée

MAKES 6

250 g/9 oz fresh strawberries,
   hulled

85 g/3 oz caster sugar

500 ml/18 fl oz whipping cream

6 egg yolks

1 teaspoon vanilla extract

For the topping

115g/4 oz caster sugar

The combination of the crisp caramel topping with the velvety strawberry cream is pure indulgence.

1. Put the oven on low: 100°/200°F/Gas ¼/fan oven 100°C.
2. Place the strawberries and 25 g/1 oz of the sugar with a tablespoon of water in a small pan and simmer gently until the berries have softened. Now, you can either purée the contents of the pan with a hand blender and pass the mixture through a sieve to remove any bits, or allow the strawberries to cool, and rub the pan contents through a sieve.
3. Mix together the cream, the remaining sugar, the egg yolks and the vanilla, then stir into it the sieved strawberry purée. Taste and, if necessary, sweeten with more sugar.
4. Pour the mixture into 6 x 150 ml/¼ pt ramekin dishes, and arrange these in a roasting tin. Pour in sufficient tap-hot water to come about two-thirds of the way up the sides of the dishes, and transfer the tin to the oven for 1½ hours.
5. Remove the tin from the oven and allow the strawberry mixture to cool. Then chill it in the coldest part of the fridge until it is firm, preferably overnight.
6. Pre-heat the grill on full blast for at least 5 minutes, so it really is red hot. Sprinkle each ramekin with caster sugar then grill them until the tops are golden brown – it happens quickly so watch them all the time. Or, of course, you could be flash and use a blow torch.
7. Leave them to cool, chill briefly, then serve. The caramel should be rock hard: don't leave them too long before serving or it will turn to liquid.

Tiramisu Profiteroles

MAKES ABOUT 3 DOZEN

A dessert to die for. This recipe takes all the ingredients you normally associate with that famous Italian dessert and uses them as a filling for profiteroles. If you like Tiramisu and you like profiteroles, then this is the one for you.

1. Pre-heat the oven to 180°C/350°F/Gas 4/fan oven 160C.
2. Make up the choux pastry according to the recipe and, using a 1-cm/½-in plain piping nozzle, pipe out blobs the size of an old 50p piece on to greased and floured trays.
3. Bake for about 30 minutes (the centres should dry out in this time). Let them cool, then cut them in half.
4. Mix the egg yolks and caster sugar together in a heat-proof bowl. Position the bowl over a pan of simmering water and whisk until the mixture is light and fluffy, about 5–8 minutes. Remove the bowl from the heat.
5. Dissolve the coffee powder in the coffee liqueur, then stir it into the egg mixture, followed by the chocolate. Give the chocolate time to melt, then stir to blend evenly.
6. Now gradually stir in the cheese – don't be afraid to beat the mixture to get rid of any lumps, but stop beating as soon as it is smooth.
7. In a separate bowl, combine the egg whites with the sugar and whisk until they are light and fluffy. Fold the whites into the mascarpone mixture and leave it on one side until you are ready to use it.
8. For the sauce, put the cream and chocolate in a small pan and warm it gently until the chocolate has melted. Then add the coffee powder. Stir until smooth, then remove the pan from the heat. You can serve it either hot or cold.
9. Fill each of the cooled profiteroles with a large spoonful of the filling and serve them with some chocolate sauce.

Note: In the restaurant I feather the dark chocolate with white chocolate.

1 quantity Choux Pastry (see page 110)

For the filling
4 egg yolks
85 g/3 oz caster sugar
1 teaspoon instant coffee powder or granules
1 tablespoon coffee liqueur
50 g/2 oz plain chocolate, chopped
350 g/12 oz mascarpone cheese, beaten until smooth
2 egg whites
25 g/1 oz caster sugar

For the chocolate sauce
300 ml/½ pt whipping cream
115 g/4 oz plain chocolate, broken in sections
1 teaspoon instant coffee powder or granules

Mille-feuille of Alcoholic Fruits

SERVES 4

175 g/6 oz puff pastry

For the meringue
2 egg whites
115 g/4 oz caster sugar
few drops of vanilla extract

For the fruit layers
350 g/12 oz fresh strawberries,
   hulled and quartered
2 tablespoons orange liqueur

To decorate
fresh sprigs of mint

The ultimate combination, which will take you to the year 2000 – crisp layers of pastry stacked with boozy fruits and layered with hot, chewy meringue. Sounds complicated, but it's easy. Here I have used strawberries, but you can use any combination of soft berries.

1. Pre-heat the oven to 200°C/400°F/Gas 6/fan oven 180°C.
2. Roll out the pastry thinly, prick it all over with a fork and bake it on a large baking tray until it is golden brown and has just slightly risen, about 10–15 minutes. Remove it from the oven, leaving the oven switched on.
3. Use a plain 9 cm/3½ in pastry cutter to cut out 12 rounds. Discard the trimmings and replace the pastry rounds on the baking tray. Keep on one side.
4. Whisk the egg whites until they are stiff, then whisk in the caster sugar slowly, a teaspoon at a time. When all the sugar has been incorporated, you should have a stiff meringue. Fold in a few drops of vanilla extract.
5. Fit a large piping bag with a rosette nozzle, fill it with the meringue and pipe an attractive border around the edge of each pastry disc. Return the tray to the oven to bake for 5 minutes or until lightly browned.
6. While the meringue is cooking, put the strawberries in a bowl and spoon the orange liqueur over them.
7. Remove the pastries from the oven and start the stacking process. Put one round on each warmed serving plate, fill the centre with strawberries. Top with another pastry layer, fill the centre with strawberries, then repeat with a final layer, three tiers in all. Continue until you have made 4 stacks. Decorate with mint leaves and serve.

After-dinner Treats

Black and White Biscuits

Crisp Almond Cigars with Strawberry and Mint Chocolate Dips

Iced Chocolates on Ashworth Moor Mist

Marzipan Shamrocks

Painter's Palette of Petits Fours

Pink Champagne and Orange Granita

Quick Rum Truffles

Rich Chocolate Squares

Rum-scented Mini Eccles Cakes

Black and White Biscuits

MAKES 24 pairs

Everybody is knocked out by the Catherine-wheel pattern of these biscuits.

1. Mix together the flour, icing sugar, butter, vanilla and egg to form a smooth dough. Divide the mixture in half.
2. To one half add the orange zest and mix in. To the other half add the cocoa and mix in. Cover both doughs with cling-film, then leave them to rest in the fridge for about an hour, or until they are firm.
3. Roll out the dark dough to a neat 24 cm/9½ in square and transfer it to a sheet of greaseproof paper. Brush it with the egg white.
4. Now roll out the orange-flavoured dough as near as possible to the same size as the dark dough. Lay the white pastry on top, cut the edges even and then roll up the dough firmly into a cigar shape, using the greaseproof paper to help you roll and keep the shape even.
5. Leaving the greaseproof paper wrapped around the dough, place the roll in the freezer for 30 minutes to harden. This makes it easier to cut into thin slices.
6. Preheat the oven to 180°C/350°F/Gas 4/fan oven 160°C.
7. When the dough is firm, cut it into slices 3–5 mm/⅛–¼ in thick and place the biscuits on lightly greased baking trays. (You will probably have to cook them in several batches.) Bake for about 10 minutes or until they are very lightly coloured and firm to the touch.
8. Remove the biscuits from the oven and leave them for about 5 minutes to harden. Use a palette knife to transfer them to a cooling rack.
9. When they are cold, pair the biscuits and sandwich them together with the chocolate and hazelnut spread, or the individual biscuits can be dipped in the spread.

250 g/9 oz plain flour, sifted

85 g/3 oz icing sugar, sifted

115 g/4 oz butter, at room temperature

½ teaspoon vanilla extract

1 egg

finely grated zest of ½ orange

1 tablespoon cocoa powder, sifted

1 egg white

1 jar chocolate and hazelnut spread

Crisp Almond Cigars with Strawberry and Mint Chocolate Dips

MAKES ABOUT 20 biscuits

For the biscuit mix
115 g/4 oz plain flour
115 g/4 oz icing sugar
100 g/3½ oz butter, melted
2 egg whites
a few drops of almond extract

For the strawberry dip
6 large strawberries, hulled
150 ml/¼ pt plain yoghurt
a little caster sugar to taste

For the mint chocolate dip
150 ml/¼ pt crème fraîche
50 g/2 oz plain chocolate,
  grated
6–8 fresh mint leaves, finely
  chopped
a little milk
a little caster sugar to taste

These biscuits are made a bit like brandy snaps. Once the thin, flat biscuits are removed from the oven, you need to work quickly, wrapping them around the handle of a wooden spoon to form the cigar shape. If they get too cold and crisp to roll, pop them back in the oven to re-heat for about 3 minutes and they'll be pliable enough to roll without becoming over-baked.

1. Pre-heat the oven to 180°C/350°F/Gas 4/fan oven 160°C.
2. Sift the flour and the icing sugar together into a bowl. Pour in the butter, the unbeaten egg whites and the almond extract, then stir to form a paste. This mix can be made 1 week in advance and stored in the fridge until needed.
3. Moisten some kitchen paper with vegetable oil and wipe this over the surface of 2 non-stick baking trays – a double insurance! Drop a teaspoon of the mixture on to the baking tray and use a small palette knife to spread the mixture thinly into rounds about 10 cm/4 in in diameter. It is best not to have more than 4 on each baking tray.
4. Bake one tray at a time, for about 5 minutes, or until the biscuits are golden brown around the edges.
5. Remove the biscuits from the oven and immediately roll them around the end of a greased wooden spoon to form a cylinder or tube. They set quickly into the shape so you can work fast – asbestos fingers are an advantage! Leave them to cool on a wire rack.
6. Quickly get the next batch into the oven, then clean and oil the first baking tray, but give it time to cool before you spread the next batch of biscuit mix. If you make 20 biscuits, you will need to do 5 batches, but don't get fazed because you will soon set up a working rhythm and the

Peach and Almond Tart with Custard Cream Ice-cream

Painter's Palette of Petits Fours

biscuits will be ready in a trice. Please note that, once made, the biscuits are best eaten within a few hours.

7. To make the strawberry dip, put the strawberries in a food processor, blend, then add the yoghurt, blend again, and add sugar to taste.

8. For the mint chocolate dip, mix the crème fraîche with the grated chocolate and mint leaves, then stir and add sufficient milk to give the same consistency as the strawberry dip. Add sugar to taste.

9. Serve the biscuits with the two complementing dips.

Iced Chocolates on Ashworth Moor Mist

MAKES ABOUT 20 chocolates

This scrumptious idea originates from Anton Edelmann, Maître Chef de Cuisine at London's prestigious Savoy Hotel. It was Edelmann who took a chance by offering me an apprenticeship at the Savoy at the tender age of sixteen. The three years I spent there were the most valuable of my career.

Once made, these ice-cream chocolates can be eaten at any time. For the most spectacular finale to a meal serve them on a bed of dry ice – which is what I call Ashworth Moor Mist.

500ml/18 fl oz container of ice-cream – it must be *firm* **scoop**

115 g/4 oz plain chocolate, melted

115 g/4 oz top-quality white chocolate, melted

1. Place a baking tray in the freezer for at least 10 minutes to get ice cold. *This is essential.*

2. Working quickly with a melon-baller, scoop out tiny balls of ice-cream and place them on the chilled baking tray. Push a cocktail stick into each ball and return them to the freezer. Leave them there until the ice-cream has set rock-hard.

3. Have the two chocolates ready melted in separate bowls. The temperature of the chocolate is all-important. It needs to be at the stage of being barely warm, but still liquid. If the chocolate is too hot, it will melt the ice-cream and slip off without coating it. If it is too cold, it will not coat the

ice-cream evenly. Dip each ice-cream ball in the chocolate, return them to the tray and replace it in the freezer. The chocolates can stay there until you are ready to serve them.

4. If you want to impress, serve the chocolates in a shallow bowl placed over some dry ice. Pour some boiling water on to the dry ice and serve straight away as the 'mist' swirls around. What a finale! (Dry ice is available from specialist gas suppliers. It's quite expensive, but if you're after a really spectacular effect it's worth it!)

Marzipan Shamrocks

MAKES 12–14

115 g/4 oz icing sugar, plus a little extra, sifted
115 g/4 oz ground almonds
1 egg white
few drops of almond extract
red and green food colouring
115 g/4 oz plain chocolate, melted

This is made up of 3 long strips of chocolate-coated almond paste which, when cut, form a coloured shamrock shape. Great to serve with coffee after a special meal, and easy enough for the kids to lend a hand.

1. Combine the icing sugar and ground almonds in a mixing bowl. Reserve a teaspoon of egg white and add the rest to the bowl with the almond extract. Stir to form a stiff paste then divide the mixture into 3 equal parts.
2. To one part, add a few drops of red food colouring and knead it in smoothly. To another part, work in a few drops of green colouring. Leave the remaining third plain.
3. Dust the work surface with just a little additional icing sugar. Use your hands to roll out each part of the almond paste to even 18-cm/7-in long sausage shapes.
4. Use the reserved egg white to brush down one side of one strip and lightly press a second strip next to it so that they lie side by side. Brush the top of the 2 strips and place the last one on top to form a triangular shape. Place it on a piece of greaseproof paper.
5. Use a brush to paint melted chocolate all over the visible surface of the almond paste and leave it to set.

6. Turn the log over to enable you to paint the underside so that the whole thing is covered in chocolate. Leave it until it has set firm.
7. Use a serrated knife to cut in 1-cm/½-in slices as and when they are required.

Painter's Palette of Petits Fours

MAKES ABOUT 6 DOZEN tiny tartlets

A spectacle of colours and tantalizing fruit. Use whatever fruit you can get your hands on, especially those in season and at their best, then arrange them in a sweep of colours that graduate from light to dark. Outside the summer months, you could use a combination of exotic fruits like mango, passion and kiwi. I know all this may sound fiddly and time-consuming, but you will be surprised at just how quickly the tartlets can be assembled for that special do when you want to show off.

1. Start with my quick pastry. Put the flour and butter in a food processor and blitz until it looks like breadcrumbs. Mix the egg yolk with the water, add it to the food processor and blitz again until the mixture comes together in a ball. Done!
2. Because of the number of tiny tartlets, use 2 x twelve-hole tartlet tins, the type used for mini muffins, and bake the bases in three batches. Roll out the pastry thinly then stamp out rounds using a 5 cm/2 in plain pastry cutter. Line the greased tartlet tins, prick each base with a fork, then refrigerate them for about 15 minutes while the oven is heating to 180°C/350°F/Gas 4/fan oven 160°C. Bake the tartlet cases for about 10 minutes, or until they are pale golden. Remove them from the oven, turn them out of the tins and leave them to cool.
3. Now make the custard. Heat the milk with the split vanilla pod to just below boiling point.
4. In a bowl, mix the egg yolks, sugar and flour to a smooth paste. Pour half the milk into the bowl, whisking all the

For the pastry
225 g/ 8 oz plain flour
115 g/4 oz butter, chilled and cubed
1 egg yolk
3 tablespoons ice-cold water

For the French custard
300 ml/½ pt milk, simmering
1 vanilla pod, split in half lengthways
3 egg yolks
50 g/2 oz caster sugar
25 g/1 oz plain flour
a sprinkling of icing sugar

For the fillings
about 450 g/1 lb mixed soft fruits, e.g. raspberries, strawberries, red and/or white currants, blackberries, blueberries
apricot jam (optional)

time. Then pour this mixture back into the milk remaining in the pan and cook over a moderate heat, stirring constantly, until the mixture has fully thickened.

5. Remove the custard from the heat, scrape it into a bowl and dust it with a little icing sugar to prevent a skin forming.

6. Once the custard has cooled, use it to fill the pastry cases. Top them with your chosen fruits. You can glaze them with a brushing of apricot jam, but it's not absolutely necessary. For a really dramatic finish, arrange the tartlets in a colour-co-ordinated way on serving trays. Wash the vanilla pod, feather one end of it so that it resembles a paintbrush and lay it alongside your creation!

Pink Champagne and Orange Granita

1 bottle pink champagne (some supermarkets' own brands are very good)
600 ml/1 pt orange juice
1 tablespoon brandy
115 g/4 oz caster sugar
juice of 1 lime
some sprigs of fresh mint, to decorate

A granita is flavoured crushed ice crystals, but that description definitely undersells the granita experience. Granitas are superb! Usually you come across one as a refreshing summer dessert, although it may be served between courses to refresh the palate. This recipe calls for pink champagne but you could use a dry pink sparkling cava wine for half the price, call it a pink champagne and orange granita when you serve it, and no one will know the difference.

1. Ideally, use a plastic freezer container that is large but shallow – for example, 23 cm/9 in square and 7.5 cm/3 in deep. This wide area gives a shallower depth of mix which freezes more quickly, and the larger surface area makes it easier to fork the ice into frozen crystals.

2. Mix all the ingredients together in a large jug and stir occasionally until the sugar has dissolved. Taste for sweetness – if need be, add a touch more sugar.

3. Pour the mixture into the freezer container and freeze it for about 6 hours, or until solid.

4. Remove from the freezer when you need it and use a large, strong fork to scrape the ice into a crushed mass. Spoon it quickly into chilled glasses, top it with a sprig of mint and serve. It's sublime.

Quick Rum Truffles

MAKES ABOUT 14

If you have any leftover cake trimmings, perhaps after making the Pineapple Baked Alaska (page 91), freeze them and use them to make these truffles. Great to have around Christmas-time and impressive to serve with coffee at the end of a dinner party. They are moist, alcoholic and moreish.

1. Combine all the ingredients for the truffles in a bowl and mix together to form a uniform paste.
2. Take small spoons of the mixture, roll it into balls and put them on a plate. Refrigerate until they are firm.
3. You can coat some of the truffles in cocoa powder: these should be rolled in the sifted powder while they are still a little soft. For the others, use a fork to dip each truffle in the melted chocolate and leave them to set on a sheet of greaseproof paper. Coat them with chopped nuts or vermicelli before the chocolate has completely set.
4. Keep them in the fridge until you want to serve them. They look good served in those dark brown sweet papers, which you can buy at a specialist stationer's.

For the truffles
50 g/2 oz cake trimmings, crumbled
50 g/2 oz icing sugar, sifted
50 g/2 oz ground almonds
1 tablespoon rum
50 g/2 oz plain chocolate, melted
1 tablespoon cream

To coat
115 g/4 oz plain chocolate, melted
chopped roasted almonds, hazelnuts, chocolate vermicelli, or sifted cocoa powder

Rich Chocolate Squares

MAKES 30

225 g/8 oz plain chocolate,
    broken into sections

175 g/6 oz butter

1 teaspoon vanilla extract

140 g/5 oz caster sugar

5 eggs

115 g/4 oz plain flour, sifted

a little icing sugar

These chocolate squares are a cross between a chewy brownie and a chocolate gâteau. The texture is pure velvet.

1. Pre-heat the oven to 120°C/250°F/Gas ½/fan oven 120°C.
2. You will need a small roasting tin, base measurement 23 x 17 cm/9 x 6½ in, or any tin that is smaller both ways by up to 3 cm/1¼ in will do. Take into account that the squares will be about 2.5 cm/1 in deep when baked. Grease the tin, then run a good spoonful of flour around the inside and tip out the excess. This will prevent the mixture sticking.
3. Put the chocolate and butter in a small pan and melt them over a low heat. Remove the pan from the heat and leave it to cool, stirring occasionally. The mixture is ready to use when the chocolate and butter combine to form a uniform consistency.
4. Put the vanilla, sugar and eggs in a large mixing bowl. Using an electric whisk, beat the mixture for 6–8 minutes until it is very pale and fluffy. Sift a little of the flour on to the mixture and gently fold it in using one of the beaters, ejected from the electric whisk. Continue in this way, folding in a little flour at a time, trying to keep as much air as possible in the mixture.
5. Now, still treating it very gently, fold in the cooled chocolate mixture, using a large spoon. When no chocolate streaks remain, pour the mixture into the tin and bake it for 30 minutes. Even if the cake looks or feels under-cooked, take it out of the oven now. The worse thing you can do is to overcook it because it will taste dry.
6. Leave it to cool for about 10 minutes then free the sides with a knife and turn it out on to a wire rack. Lay another rack on top and turn it over so that the cake is top side up. Dust it liberally with icing sugar. When it is cold cut it into small squares.

Rum-scented Mini Eccles Cakes

MAKES ABOUT 16

A great wicked twist on the normal. Marinate the currants in your favourite spirit for 24 hours and you're in for a treat. You can use any spirit, rum, brandy or whisky, but the combination of orange liqueur and zest seems to work particularly well. Don't forget that these are intended as after dinner treats so they are made small; each Eccles is one mouthful, two at the most.

115 g/ 4 oz currants

4 tablespoons orange liqueur

finely grated zest of ½ orange

175 g/6 oz puff pastry – use
  trimmings, if you like

25 g/1 oz butter

a little caster sugar for
  sprinkling

1 egg, beaten

1. Combine the currants, orange liqueur and zest in a small bowl, cover and leave for 24 hours, or until the fruit is plump and has absorbed the liqueur.
2. Pre-heat the oven to 160°C/325°F/Gas 3/fan oven 140°C.
3. Roll out the puff pastry until it is nice and thin (it's a good way to use pastry trimmings as you don't need the pastry to rise) and then cut it into rounds the size of a tumbler, about 6–7 cm/2½–2¾ in diameter.
4. Place a scant teaspoonful of marinated currants in the middle and add a small piece of butter and a sprinkle of sugar. Brush the outer edge of the pastry with the egg, then gather the pastry rim together in the centre and pinch to seal the filling in a small pastry sack.
5. Turn the Eccles cake so that the sealed bit is underneath, then roll it gently with a rolling pin, just until the fruit starts to show beneath the pastry and the cake is slightly flattened. Continue until the ingredients are used up.
6. Place the cakes on a baking sheet and brush the tops with a touch more egg. Dust with sugar and make a cut in the top of each cake.
7. Put them in the oven for about 10 minutes or until they are golden brown.
8. Remove them from the oven, cool them slightly and serve.

Basic Recipes

Basic Sponge

MAKES 2 x 18-cm/7-in round sandwich cakes

Sorry, folks, but unless you have muscles and Olympic endurance, you will need an electric whisk for this sponge. You can use one sponge round right away and the other can be wrapped closely in cling-film, sealed in a plastic bag and frozen, ready for use in emergencies.

4 eggs

115 g/4 oz caster sugar

1 teaspoon vanilla extract

115 g/4 oz plain flour, sifted

1. Pre-heat the oven to 180°C/350°F/Gas 4/fan oven 160°C. Grease and line 2 x 18-cm/7-in round sandwich tins with greaseproof paper or baking parchment. Grease the paper.
2. Combine the eggs, sugar and vanilla in a large mixing bowl. Use an electric whisk to beat the ingredients until the mixture is light, almost white and fluffy; it should take 5–6 minutes.
3. Sift in the flour. Now, here's a good tip: eject the beaters from the electric whisk and use one to gently fold the flour in. The aim is to incorporate the flour smoothly while keeping as much air as possible in the mixture.
4. Divide the mixture equally between the tins, then bake for 15 minutes or until the cakes are golden brown, well risen and springy to touch when tested in the centre.
5. Remove them from the oven and leave them to cool for a minute or two. Turn out on to your oven-gloved hand and quickly strip off the lining papers. Lay a wire rack gently on the base of the cake and turn the rack and the cake over so that the cake comes to rest on the wire rack, top side up. If you do it this way, you won't get the impression of the wire rack on top of the cake. Once they are cold, the cakes are ready for use.

Choux Pastry

300 ml/½ pt water

115 g/4 oz butter, cubed

140 g/5 oz plain flour, sifted

4 eggs

1. In a medium-size pan, preferably non-stick, bring the water to the boil. Add the butter and boil gently until it has melted.
2. Remove the pan from the heat and immediately beat in the flour until the mixture forms a thick, smooth paste. Return the pan to a low heat and continue to beat for about 1 minute. Now remove the pan from the heat and leave the mixture to cool for about 5 minutes.
3. Add the eggs, one at a time, beating well between each addition. The mixture will then be a shiny paste just stiff enough to hold a shape.
4. If you don't want to use it immediately, transfer the paste to a bowl, cover it with cling-film and refrigerate for up to 24 hours.

Chicken Stock

MAKES ABOUT 1 L/1¾ pt

1.5 kg/3½ lb raw chicken bones

2 carrots, peeled and coarsely chopped

2 celery sticks, cut in chunks

1 large leek, trimmed, washed and coarsely chopped

1 onion, peeled and stuck with 2–3 cloves

1 bay leaf

several sprigs thyme and parsley

some unpeeled garlic cloves, if appropriate

Is it just my imagination, or are those frozen packs of chicken giblets disappearing from the supermarkets? And 'boiling fowls' are definitely a thing of the past. But there is nothing to beat a home-made chicken stock, so here is a recipe for a light chicken stock using raw chicken bones. These can be saved in the freezer until you have enough to make a stock or, if you are feeling flush, use packets of chicken wings and give the meat to the cat.

1. Put the bones in a large, deep pan, cover generously with cold water and bring to the boil. Skim off any scum that collects on the surface.
2. Add the rest of the ingredients to the pan and adjust the heat to give a gentle simmer. Leave to cook for about 4 hours. Taste and see if the stock has a good flavour, bearing in mind any recipe for which you may intend to use it.
3. Strain the stock through a fine sieve into a large bowl, cool then refrigerate overnight.

4. The following day, discard any fat that has formed on the surface. If you are not using the stock immmediately, decant it into an old clean mineral-water bottle. Don't fill it to the top, because the stock will expand as it freezes. Label and freeze it until you are ready to use it.

Fish Stock

MAKES ABOUT 1 L/1¾ pt

A good stock to give background flavour to a recipe without being too strong or dominant. Freeze all the white fish bones that come your way and, when you have enough, make them into stock and freeze it. Avoid using herring and mackerel bones, and don't cook the stock too long or weird flavours will develop.

1. Put all the fish trimmings in a colander and wash them under cold running water. Transfer them to a large pan and add the remaining ingredients. Pour in sufficient cold water to cover.
2. Bring to the boil, skimming off any scum that forms on the surface. Adjust the heat to a gentle simmer and cook for 20 minutes.
3. Strain the contents of the pan through a fine sieve and leave the stock to cool. Use within 24 hours or freeze in used clean mineral-water bottles. Don't fill the bottles completely because the liquid will expand as it freezes – and don't forget to label them.

450 g/1 lb fish trimmings
1 small onion, peeled and
  thickly sliced
1 small stick celery, coarsely
  chopped
a few parsley stalks
sprig of fresh thyme
1 bay leaf
a few black peppercorns
strip of lemon peel

Vegetable Stock

MAKES ABOUT 1 L/1¾ pt

1 onion, peeled and finely
    chopped
1 leek, trimmed, chopped and
    washed
2 carrots, peeled and chopped
½ bulb fennel, finely chopped
2 sticks celery, finely chopped
2 cloves garlic, peel left on,
    crushed
several sprigs of thyme
1 bay leaf
good handful parsley stalks
½ lemon, sliced
125 ml/4 fl oz dry white wine

Vegetable stocks vary enormously in flavour, so experiment a bit, but my advice is to go easy on the herbs. Also, I prefer to chop the vegetables finely and cook them for a short time, rather than chop coarsely and cook four times longer. Chop them in the food processor for speed.

1. Put all of the vegetables into a large pan with the thyme and bay leaf. Pour in 1 L/1¾ pt cold water. Bring to the boil and simmer for 12–15 minutes. Now add the parsley and lemon. Bring the stock back to the boil and remove the pan from the heat. Cover and leave it overnight.
2. The following day strain the stock through a fine sieve and stir in the wine. Store covered, in the fridge, for up to 3 days, or freeze as for Chicken Stock (see page 110).

Quick Hollandaise Sauce

3 egg yolks
2 tablespoons lemon juice *or*
    white wine vinegar
salt and freshly ground black
    pepper
115 g/4 oz butter, bubbling hot

This is a speedy variation on the classic method. It gives a slightly more runny sauce with less bite, but a lot of people prefer it. The bubbling hot butter is crucial to the sauce: its heat 'cooks' the egg yolks and makes the sauce thicken.

1. Put the egg yolks and lemon juice or vinegar into a food processor, season and set the machine in motion.
2. Have the butter bubbling hot on the heat. Take the pan off the heat and pour it on to the whirling food processor blades in a thin stream, then leave to blend for about 30 seconds until the sauce has thickened and is foamy. Season to taste before serving.

Mayonnaise

MAKES 300 ml/½ pt

Since the arrival of food processors in the kitchen, mayonnaise can be made in minutes. I have given a pretty basic recipe below, but you can add to it in any way you like. For a really sharp flavour use lime juice instead of the vinegar or lemon juice, and I often throw in the grated zest of the lime at the end.

1. Put the whole egg and the egg yolk, and the mustard, vinegar or lemon juice in a food processor with some seasoning. Start the machine.
2. Have the oil ready in a jug and start to pour a thin trickle of oil on to the blades while the machine is running. Once the mayonnaise shows definite signs of thickening, you can add the oil a little faster.
3. When all the oil has been added, stop the machine and season the mayonnaise to taste, making sure that the flavour will balance with the food with which it is to be served. You can keep it in a sealed container in the fridge for about 1 week.

I whole egg plus I yolk
½ teaspoon Dijon mustard
2 tablespoons white wine
  vinegar or lemon juice
salt and freshly ground black
  pepper
300 ml/½ pt oil, half olive, half
  groundnut or sunflower

Nutter's Utterly Nutty Menus

This collection of menus is based around the *Utter Nutter* television series, in which each programme centred on an exciting theme, be it fire, flames or even illusions. The concept was such a success that I thought you might like to try my menu ideas for a themed evening with a difference.

With each menu I suggest that you drink your favourite white or red wine, but I have included an array of exciting cocktails, put together by Andrew Wringe from Continental and Overseas Wines, to get the evening off to an utterly nutty start. They are really wicked cocktails which you must try!

Go on – be like Nutter and go totally mad with these utterly nutty menus!

Black and White

This jazz-inspired menu comprises anything black and white – for that total impact, go for colour-co-ordinated plates, flowers and table settings.

Cauliflower and Roquefort Soup with Jet Black Crostini

Poached Cod with Squid Ink Tagliatelle

Black and White Minstrel Cheesecake

COCKTAILS

BLACK VELVET

Mix a third of Guinness with two-thirds champagne in a pint glass.

BABY GUINNESS

Pour a measure of Tia Maria into a liqueur glass. Then add half a measure of Bailey's Irish Cream, which should float on top.

Water

Blue's the theme for this menu, and fish the order of the day.

Shellfish Soup with Garlic and Basil Paste

Brill with Potato Scales and Tomato-scented Cous-cous

Choux Swans on a Strawberry Lake

Rum-scented Mini Eccles Cakes

COCKTAIL

BARRIER REEF
2 measures gin
1 measure Triple Sec
⅓ measure Grand Marnier
½ measure Blue Curaçao
4 tablespoons vanilla ice-cream
maraschino cherries, pineapple, orange
Blend all the ingredients briefly in a liquidizer and pour into an ice-filled piña colada glass.
Garnish with maraschino cherries, slices of pineapple and a slice of orange.
Serve with thick straws.

Fire and Flames

Lots of action here with flames of brandy and red-hot food – so have that fire extinguisher ready just in case.

Seared Cherry Tomato and Roast Garlic Soup

Red Mullet with a Fiery Hot Mango and Coriander Salsa

Peppered Steak with Mushroom Mash

Strawberry Crème Brûlée

COCKTAIL

FLAME THROWER
¾ measure grappa
¾ measure Southern Comfort
1 teaspoon white rum
Pour the grappa and the Southern Comfort into a glass.
Heat the rum in a teaspoon, ignite then add it flaming to the glass,
blow out the flame and drink immediately.

Passion

It's a romantic dinner so get the candles out, dim those lights and have the champagne chilling. Love is in the air!

Mushroom Soup

Asparagus and Parma Ham Salad

Herb-crusted Salmon with a Champagne Sauce

Chilled Delicate Chocolate Desserts

Main drink: champagne, of course.

COCKTAIL

PASSION PUNCH
1½ measures golden rum
1 measure red grape juice
1 measure passion fruit juice
1 measure pineapple juice
Mix all the ingredients in a jug with a glassful of crushed ice and serve in champagne glasses.

The Future

This menu is out of this world – think X Files, Mission Impossible
and get those lasers out!

Crostini with Three Toppings

White Stilton Waffles with Tangy Rocket Leaves

Futuristic Fish and Chips

Banoffee Treasure Chest

COCKTAIL

PAN-GALACTIC GARGLE BLASTER

This cocktail is made famous by the book and radio play,
A Hitchhiker's Guide to the Galaxy.
1½ measures melon liqueur
½ measure overproof white rum
½ measure fresh lime juice
½ measure pineapple juice
1½ measures lemonade
Mix the first four ingredients together and shake with ice. Strain on to ice, and add the lemonade.

Illusions

This menu concentrates on dishes that aren't what they seem. Go for bright and colourful table settings because the food is lively and energetic.

Smoked Haddock and Spring Onion Risotto

Pork Pieces with Melting Stilton and Chive Fondue

Hot Chocolate Pizza

Painter's Palette of Petit Fours

COCKTAILS

DRAMBUIE SHOT

Pour 1 measure Drambuie into a brandy glass and ignite. Once the liquor is flaming place your hand over the glass and, as if by magic, the flame disappears but the glass sticks to your hand! Shake it around – look, no hands! Remove your hand and drink in one.

THE ILLUSION

1 measure Kahlua

1 measure Midori

1 measure Bailey's Irish Cream

Pour the Kahlua over a teaspoon into a small glass. Do exactly the same with the Midori and follow with the Bailey's Irish Cream. They should rest on top of one another.

Speed

Choose this menu if you haven't lots of time or if guests have suddenly appeared.

Pea and Fennel Soup

Flash-seared Salmon with a Cucumber and Dill Dressing

Chicken with Ginger and Spring Onions

Pineapple Baked Alaska

COCKTAILS

SILVER STREAK
1 measure Kummel
1 measure gin
Shake the Kummel and gin together with some crushed ice.
Then strain into a dry martini glass and flavour with caraway.

FERRARI
1 measure Amaretto
2 measures Cinzano Dry
Shake the Amaretto and Cinzano vigorously with some crushed ice.
Pour into a glass.

Explosions

A totally wacky menu with lots of unusual happenings. Have some fireworks ready for that ultimate finale to the evening.

Crispy Bury Black Pudding Won-tons

Dazzling Duck with a Honey and Mustard Glaze

Chocolate and Banana Timbales with a Liquid Chocolate Centre

Iced Chocolate on Ashworth Moor Mist

COCKTAIL

BANANA BOMBSHELL

1½ measures white rum

1 measure crème de banane

1 measure coconut cream

1 measure sugar syrup

1 measure whipping cream

4 measures pineapple juice

⅓ banana, mashed

Put all the ingredients into a blender with some ice and process until smooth. Pour into a large glass and garnish with slices of pineapple, a couple of cherries, and a slice of lemon with excess peel dangling over the side of the glass like a fuse.

Index

Metric Conversion Chart

Based on the Guild of Food Writers Metric Conversions

WEIGHT

Metric	Imperial
15 g	$\frac{1}{2}$ oz
20 g	$\frac{3}{4}$ oz
25 g	1 oz
35 g	$1\frac{1}{4}$ oz
40 g	$1\frac{1}{2}$ oz
50 g	$1\frac{3}{4}$ oz
55 g	2 oz
60 g	$2\frac{1}{4}$ oz
70 g	$2\frac{1}{2}$ oz
75 g	$2\frac{3}{4}$ oz
85 g	3 oz
90 g	$3\frac{1}{4}$ oz
100 g	$3\frac{1}{2}$ oz
115 g	4 oz
125 g	$4\frac{1}{2}$ oz
140 g	5 oz
150 g	$5\frac{1}{2}$ oz
175 g	6 oz
190 g	$6\frac{1}{2}$ oz
200 g	7 oz
215 g	$7\frac{1}{2}$ oz
225 g	8 oz
240 g	$8\frac{1}{2}$ oz
250 g	9 oz
275 g	$9\frac{1}{2}$ oz
280 g	10 oz
300 g	$10\frac{1}{2}$ oz
315 g	11 oz
325 g	$11\frac{1}{2}$ oz
350 g	12 oz
365 g	$12\frac{1}{2}$ oz
375 g	13 oz
400 g	14 oz
425 g	15 oz
450 g	1 lb
500 g	1 lb 2 oz
550 g	1 lb 4 oz
600 g	1 lb 5 oz
650 g	1 lb 7 oz
700 g	1 lb 9 oz
750 g	1 lb 10 oz
800 g	1 lb 12 oz
850 g	1 lb 14 oz
900 g	2 lb
955 g	2 lb 2 oz
1 kg	2 lb 4 oz
1.25 kg	2 lb 12 oz
1.3 kg	3 lb
1.5 kg	3 lb 5 oz
1.6 kg	3 lb 8 oz
1.82 kg	4 lb
2 kg	4 lb 8 oz
2.25 kg	5 lb
2.5 kg	5 lb 8 oz
2.7 kg	6 lb
3 kg	6 lb 8 oz

VOLUME

Metric	Imperial
15 ml	$\frac{1}{2}$ fl oz
30 ml	1 fl oz
50 ml	2 fl oz
75 ml	$2\frac{1}{2}$ fl oz
100 ml	$3\frac{1}{2}$ fl oz
125 ml	4 fl oz
150 ml	5 fl oz / $\frac{1}{4}$ pint
175 ml	6 fl oz
200 ml	7 fl oz / $\frac{1}{3}$ pint
225 ml	8 fl oz
250 ml	9 fl oz
300 ml	10 fl oz / $\frac{1}{2}$ pint
350 ml	12 fl oz
400 ml	14 fl oz
425 ml	15 fl oz / $\frac{3}{4}$ pint
450 ml	16 fl oz
500 ml	18 fl oz
600 ml	20 fl oz / 1 pint
568 ml	1 pint milk
700 ml	$1\frac{1}{4}$ pint
850 ml	$1\frac{1}{2}$ pint
1 litre	$1\frac{3}{4}$ pint
1.2 litres	2 pint
1.3 litres	$2\frac{1}{4}$ pint
1.4 litres	$2\frac{1}{2}$ pint
1.5 litres	$2\frac{3}{4}$ pint
1.7 litres	3 pint
2 litres	$3\frac{1}{2}$ pint
2.5 litres	$4\frac{1}{2}$ pint
2.8 litres	5 pint
3 litres	$5\frac{1}{4}$ pint

SPOONS

Metric	Imperial
1.25 ml	$\frac{1}{4}$ tsp
2.5 ml	$\frac{1}{2}$ tsp
5 ml	1 tsp
10 ml	2 tsp
15 ml	1 tbsp/3 tsp
30 ml	2 tbsp
45 ml	3 tbsp
60 ml	4 tbsp
75 ml	5 tbsp
90 ml	6 tbsp

LINEAR

Metric	Imperial
2 mm	$\frac{1}{16}$ in
3 mm	$\frac{1}{8}$ in
5 mm	$\frac{1}{4}$ in
8 mm	$\frac{3}{8}$ in
10 mm/1 cm	$\frac{1}{2}$ in
15 mm	$\frac{5}{8}$ in
2 cm	$\frac{3}{4}$ in
2.5 cm	1 in
3 cm	$1\frac{1}{4}$ in
4 cm	$1\frac{1}{2}$ in
4.5 cm	$1\frac{3}{4}$ in
5 cm	2 in
5.5 cm	$2\frac{1}{4}$ in
6 cm	$2\frac{1}{2}$ in
7 cm	$2\frac{3}{4}$ in
7.5 cm	3 in
8.5 cm	$3\frac{1}{4}$ in
9 cm	$3\frac{1}{2}$ in
9.5 cm	$3\frac{3}{4}$ in
10 cm	4 in
11 cm	$4\frac{1}{4}$ in
12 cm	$4\frac{1}{2}$ in
13 cm	5 in
14 cm	$5\frac{1}{2}$ in
15 cm	6 in
16 cm	$6\frac{1}{4}$ in
17 cm	$6\frac{1}{2}$ in
18 cm	7 in
19 cm	$7\frac{1}{2}$ in
20 cm	8 in
22 cm	$8\frac{1}{2}$ in
23 cm	9 in
24 cm	$9\frac{1}{2}$ in
25 cm	10 in
26 cm	$10\frac{1}{2}$ in
27 cm	$10\frac{3}{4}$ in
28 cm	11 in
29 cm	$11\frac{1}{2}$ in
30 cm	12 in
31 cm	$12\frac{1}{4}$ in
33 cm	13 in
34 cm	$13\frac{1}{2}$ in
35 cm	$13\frac{3}{4}$ in
37 cm	$14\frac{1}{2}$ in
38 cm	15 in
39 cm	$15\frac{1}{4}$ in
40 cm	16 in
42 cm	$16\frac{1}{2}$ in
43 cm	17 in
44 cm	$17\frac{1}{2}$ in
46 cm	18 in
48 cm	19 in
50 cm	20 in